諦聽

林明理著

文史哲英譯叢刊

文史哲出版社印行

國家圖書館出版品預行編目資料

諦聽 / 林明理著. -- 初版 -- 臺北市：文史哲，
民 107.02
　　頁；　公分（文史哲英譯叢刊；5）
ISBN 978-986-314-401-4（平裝）

851.486　　　　　　　　　　　　107002152

文史哲英譯叢刊　　5

諦　　聽

著　　者：林　　　明　　　理
出 版 者：文　史　哲　出　版　社
http://www.lapen.com.tw
e-mail：lapen@ms74.hinet.net
登記證字號：行政院新聞局版臺業字五三三七號
發 行 人：彭　　　正　　　雄
發 行 所：文　史　哲　出　版　社
印 刷 者：文　史　哲　出　版　社
臺北市羅斯福路一段七十二巷四號
郵政劃撥帳號：一六一八〇一七五
電話886-2-23511028・傳真886-2-23965656

定價新臺幣五二〇元 彩色版一二八〇元

二〇一八年（民一〇七）二月初版

諦　聽

二、2017年詩作（2017 poems）&painting works

三、法國詩人 Athanase Vantchev de Thracy 翻譯成法詩 (French poet Athanase Vantchev de Thracy translated into poetry)

四、義大利名詩人 Giovanni Campisi 以義大利語詩給林明理詩歌 3 首

五、醫師詩人 Prof. Ernesto Kahan（獲 1985 年諾貝爾和平獎） Mail Lin Mingli 的英詩及西班牙詩歌語二首

六、附錄 appendix

2017 年英譯詩作，大部分由 Dr.William Marr 非馬英譯
2017 English transla tion of poetry & painting works
Most of them were translated by Dr. William Marr

林明理《諦聽》彩繪作品

Author : Dr.Lin Ming Li《*Listen*》

＊ Painted works ＊

LIBRARY OF CONGRESS

Asian and Middle Eastern Division
China Section
101 Independence Ave., SE
Washington, D.C. 20540-4221
Tel: (202) 707-7960
Fax: (202) 252-3354
Email: bohc@loc.gov

Date: April 25, 2017

Dr. Lin Ming-Li
No. 1, Section 2
Hsing An Road
Taitung 95058
TAIWAN

Dear Mr. Lin:

Pursuant to the authority delegated to me by the Librarian of Congress, I accept and acknowledge the receipt of the material mentioned below. We greatly appreciate your kindness in sending this material to our library.

Once again, thank you for considering the Library of Congress.

Sincerely,

Beatrice C. Ohta
Section Head

The material received:

我的歌. 2017

1.諦聽

2.畫--因為你

3.畫 M.L 詩-炫目的綠色世界

4.給 LUCY 藍晶照-明理攝

5.玉山頌，雪

6.M.L 春歸 -

7.企鵝 M.L PAINT

8. 啟示　　　Dr.Lin Mingli/painting

9.布農之歌 M.L　畫

10.黃昏的福州山

11.致 KALANIT

12.黃昏

13. 平靜的湖面　　MingLi/photo

14.冥想

15.封仔餅

16.致 Dr.珍古德

17.白冷圳之戀

18.棕熊

19.林田山之歌

20.詩與白冷圳的間奏曲

21.致詩人——Prof. Ernesto Kahan

22.致生態導演——李學主

23.憶

24.給 Ernesto Kahan 的祝禱

25.鵝鑾鼻　燈塔　　　　　26.吐瓦魯的悲歌

27.黑面琵鷺　　　　　　28

28

28.迷人的雕像──TO PROF.ERNESTO KAHAN

29.致追夢的勇士──Jennifer Bricker

30. 2017.6.8 MING-LI 義大利獎狀

  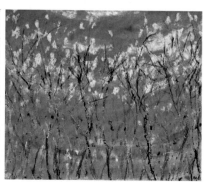

31. 2017.6.10.MING-LI PAINTGiovanni　　32 悼——空拍大師齊柏林

33. 金風鈴

34. 2017.6.23
ML 亞特蘭大
新聞詩二首
→

34.2017.6.14.MING-LI PAINT DR.WILLIAM MARR 非馬

35.一則警訊　　　　　　　36.M.L PAINT-

37. 2017.6.18 MLPAINT-FOR ERNESTO　　38. 花

39.秋的懷念　　　　　　　40.M.L 雲豹

41.我的夢想　　42. 2017.6.17.M.L PAINT　　43. 17.8.4MINGLI POEM3 亞特蘭大新聞

44.2017.6.20.ML PAINT ERNESTO　　45.2017.6.23ML PAINT

46.卡法薩巴　　47.2017.6.25 純白海灣

48.2017.6.27MLPAINT 山魈

49.2017.6.29ML PAINT-山斑馬

50. 湖泊 1MLPAINT

51.MINGLI PAINT 梅花鹿

52.山的呢喃

53. ML PAINT 萬國教堂

54.西牆

57. MINGLI-PAINTAthanase Vantchev de Thracy   58.雷鳥

63.- 詩河   64.P_AINT 銀背黑猩猩

66.馬丘比丘之頌   67. LI-美洲獅

68.-黃茂己老師

69.北非獅

70.聖母大殿 Basilica di Santa Maria Maggiore

71.火車爺爺

74.冬之歌

75.帕德嫩神廟

76.塞哥維亞舊城

77.巨石陣

78. 寂靜的遠山

79.-科隆大教堂

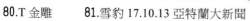

80.T 金雕　　81.雪豹 17.10.13 亞特蘭大新聞　82. 17.10.27 亞特蘭大新聞

未譯詩部份

1.春在溟濛處

2. 春語

3.安義的春天

4.在風中，寫你的名字

6.你的話語

5.幸福的火龍果

7. 桃花

8.明理畫海

9. 圖荷

10 圖蓮

11.-春之歌

12.珍珠的水田

13.海廢危機

15.牡丹水庫即景

15.牡丹水庫即景

23.致爾泰

散文:.物理界怪傑－周建和

24.2017.10.25MINGLI- TAIPEI

22. 包公

25. 傅園

2017.6.12 義大利詩人喬凡尼
提名明理諾貝爾獎

海影，2013.11.18 人間福報

散文：母子情

2017 諦 聽

1. 諦聽

小小島嶼，
無論悲傷或美麗，永遠擁抱著大海。
那歷史的斷片，撩撥我的思古。

－2017.1.13

Lin Mingli/painting

1. Listen

*Dr.Lin Ming-Li

Small islands,
Sad or beautiful, always embrace the sea.
The fragments of history, deeply provoke my thoughts.

－2017.1.13

（Translator：Dr.William Marr 非馬 英譯）

－英譯刊美國（Poems of the world）季刊，
  2016 冬季號，頁 9.
－中英譯刊美國《亞特蘭大新聞》，
  2017.1.20.圖文

2 因為你

多麼想
以垂天之翼
　輕輕地穿越時空
在你飛向遠方之前
我不再畏懼未來
因為你比我勇敢
　所以我會飛得更高
會有不同的發現和感動
　　　　－2017.01.12

Mingli/painting

2 Because of you

*Dr.Lin Ming-Li

How I would like
To fly gently through time and space
With my wings
Before you fly into the distance

I no longer fear the future
Because you are　braver than me
With all sort of discoveries and inspirations
I am sure I'll fly much higher

－2017.1.12

（Ttanslator：Dr.William Marr　非馬　英譯）

－中英譯刊美國《亞特蘭大新聞》，
2017.1.20.圖文

3. 炫目的綠色世界

大黑麥田，農場和馬房
　　從空曠到金色的海面
我無法一一盛裝
翩翩而來的春天
就像思鄉的弦懸在耳畔

　　　　　－2017.1.13

　　　　　－中英譯刊美國《亞特蘭大新聞》，
　　　　　　2017.1.27.圖文

Mingli/painting

3. The dazzling green world

*Dr.Lin Ming-Li

Large black wheat fields, farms and stables
From the open to the golden sea
I can not dress them up one by one
Spring on her dancing feet
Is like homesickness ringing in the ears

−2017.1.13

（Ttanslator：Dr.William Marr 非馬　英譯）

−英譯刊美國（POEMS OF THE WORLD）
季刊，2016 冬季號，頁 41.

4. 給 LUCY

讓我們一起詠嘆吧

那是山海交織的頌曲

妳側了身，像顆不願夢醒的朝露

— 2077.1.15 作

Mingli/photo

4. To Lucy

*Dr.Lin Ming-Li

Let's sing together
Of mountains and the sea
You turn your body, like a morning dew
Unwilling to wake up from its dream

－2017.1.15

（Ttanslator：Dr.William Marr 非馬 英譯）

－中英譯刊美國《亞特蘭大新聞》，
2017.1.20.圖文。

5. 玉山頌

站在雪地上，仰望、傾聽。
我期待你的歌聲，堅毅
深情如母親河。

—2017.1.16

（新聞報導，臺灣最高峰的玉山下了第一
場雪，因而為詩。）

Dr.LinMingli/painting

5. Ode to Yushan

*Dr.Lin Ming-Li

Standing on the snow, looking up, listening.
I look forward to hearing your strong voice
Affectionate as the mother river.

一 2017.1.16

(Recently, Taiwan's highest peak of Yushan
had its first snowfall.)

（Ttanslator：Dr.William Marr 非馬 英譯）

一 2017.1.16

一 刊美國（POEMS OF THE WORLD）季
刊，2016 冬季號，頁 3.
一 中英譯刊美國《亞特蘭大新聞》，
2017.1.27.圖文。

6. 春歸

轉瞬間
雪變成了馥郁的季節
我在草綠間尋覓
飛掠而過的蝶影
吻走最後一滴星淚

—2017.1.24

LinMingli/painting

6. *The Returning of Spring*

*Dr. Lin Ming-Li

In an instant
I find the snow has become a season of fragrance
In the green grass I look for
The shadows of flying Butterflies
Which will kiss away the last teardrop from the stars

－by 2017.1.24

（Ttanslator：Dr.William Marr 非馬　英譯）

－中英譯刊美國《亞特蘭大新聞》，2017.2.3.
圖文

7. 企鵝的悲歌

在融解的冰層上

小小企鵝扭擺著身軀，茫然地徘徊

牠昂首呼喊，發出悲鳴，劃破寂靜的雪原

—by 2017.2.1

註.報載，南極出現生態慘劇，大型冰層將
阿德利企鵝困在家園，150,000 隻企鵝因
而踏上不歸路。

Lin Mingli/painting

7. The Elegy of the Penguin

*Dr.Lin Mingli

On the melting ice,
A little penguin twists its body, wandering at a loss
It raises its head and utters a long, sad shout, piercing
the silent snowfield

―by 2017.2.1

（Ttanslator：Dr.William Marr 非馬英譯）

―中英譯刊美國《亞特蘭大新聞》，
2017.3.17.圖文。

8. 啟示

我相信是金字塔
擔心週遭的氣候暖化
悄悄地將密碼回撥太空

—2017.2.3

註：據報導，近年來全球金字塔中有幾處
出現一縷光束筆直射向外太空，科學
家指出金字塔與光子雲有不可思議的
聯繫，究竟是什麼啟動了這些金字塔
的神秘力量？令人好奇，因而為詩。

Dr.Lin Mingli/painting

8. Revelation

* Dr.Lin Mingli

I believe it was the pyramid
Worrying about the climate warming of its surrounding
Quietly sent messages to the outer space

－2017.2.3

*According to news reports, in recent years,
several pyramids in the world have shot
rays of light straight to the outer
space. Scientists pointed out that

（Ttanslator：Dr.William Marr 非馬　英譯）

－刊臺灣《臺灣時報》，2017.3.15.圖文
－中英譯刊美國《亞特蘭大新聞》2017.3.3
　圖文

9. 布農之歌

我聽過一種古謠
　　歌聲迴盪
彷彿親吻愛情的哀愁
當夜空俯視整個部落
　　辰星環抱時
浮掠而過的月光
亮成遊子的孤獨
　　坐聽布農樂舞

－2017.2.16
*此歌來自阿里山鄉來吉部落的布農族。

Lin Mingli/painting

9. Song of Bunun

* Dr.Lin Mingli

I hear a ballad
Its echoing sound
　　Seems to kiss the sorrowful love
The stars on the night sky
Surround and embrace the tribal village
While the moonlight
　　Shines on a lonely wanderer
Who is listening to Bunun's dancing music

－2017.2.16
*Bunun, a tribe of the Ali Township in Taiwan.

－刊美國《亞特蘭大新聞》，2017.2.24.
圖文。
－刊臺灣(華文現代詩)，第 13 期，2017.05.
頁 72.

10. 黃昏的福州山

寒風瑟瑟
周圍是輕拂而過的
蘆葦、花香、鳥鳴
我從未忘記
大台北熟悉的面容
也未曾回避過
生命的每一次悸動

那些年少的純真
忽而被風撩起
啊，朋友
何時再會，一起咀嚼黃昏
當燈火點綴著城市
恰如雨落風過
生活得簡單，蠻好

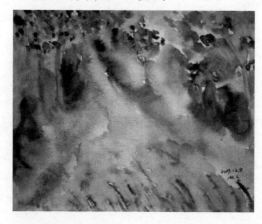

Lin Mingli/painting

10. *Dusk on Fuzhou Mountain*

* Dr.Lin Mingli

Chilly
Surrounded by flickering
Reeds, floral fragrances, birdsongs
I never forget
The familiar face of the great Taipei
And I have never missed
Any throb of life

The wind suddenly brought back
Our innocent youth
O, my friend
When will we get together to chew at dusk
When the lights dotted the city
Like the passing rain and wind
Life is simple, and nice

－刊臺灣（華文現代詩）季刊，第 13 期，
　2017.5.頁 72.
－刊臺灣《臺灣時報》，台灣文學版，圖
　文，2017.3.2.
－2017.2.14

11. 致 KALANIT

你的緋紅在風之上飛舞
是我心盤旋不去的歌
年年開在老城的各個角落
開在乾旱的沙漠
賜予以色列人民歡欣
讓大地變得如此美好

－2017.2.14

*2017.2.14Prof.Ernesto Kahan mail to me
and said "KALANIT, the national flower of Israel. Now is
the time for it flourishing."

11. To KALANIT

* Dr.Lin Mingli

Dancing in the wind, the crimson flower
Is a song hovering over my heart
Blooming every year at every corner of the ancient city
Blooming in the arid desert
A joyous gift to the people of Israel
that makes the earth so wonderful

－2017.2.14

（Ttanslator：Dr.William Marr 非馬　英譯）

－中英譯刊美國《亞特蘭大新聞》，
2017.2.17，圖文。

12. 黃　昏

越過綠野和海洋
我找到夕陽最後深情地一閃
正如四月桐鑲著雲彩
隱蔽於坡谷之下

　　　　　　－2017.2.20

Lin Mingli/painting

12. Dusk

* Dr.Lin Mingli

Over the green field and the ocean
I found the setting sun's final flash of affection
As in April, the tung tree in the valley
was put into a frame of colorful clouds

−2017.2.20

−刊臺灣（海星詩刊），第 24 期，2017.06
夏季號。

13. 平靜的湖面

在淡淡白色煙霧裡
你是思索中的詩人
看落葉褪盡
季節輪換的容貌

－2017.2.23

－刊台灣（秋水詩刊），第 172 期，2017.07.
頁 41.

MingLi/photo

13.　A Calm Lake

* Dr.Lin Mingli

In the pale fog
You are a poet in deep thought
Watching the leaves fading away
The changing face of a new season

－2017.2.23

（TRANSLATOR：DR.WILLIAM MARR
非馬　英譯）

*2017.7.17 於 8:07 AMMAIL
法國名詩人翻譯家 *Athanase Vantchev de Thracy*
翻譯此詩成法語

*2017.7.17 at 8:07 AMMAIL

French poet translator Athanase Vantchev de
Thracy Translate this poem into French

My dear Ming-Li,

Thank you for your nice picture and your poem
I translated into French：

Poème dédié au poète Athanase Vantchev de
Thracy

13.　Un lac calme

Au milieu du pâle brouillard,
Vous êtes le poète plongé dans des pensées profondes
Suivant du regard les feuilles qui s'évanouissent
Et la face de la nouvelle saison qui s'avance.

Translated into French by Athanase Vantchev de Thracy

14. 冥 想

多思慕你
　邊馳騁，邊微笑
像飛魚在水花間躍動
這是因為有普羅旺斯
　夏日才這般夢幻
還是山丘上那片愛情花海
讓我斜倚著，向宇宙說話

―2017.2.24

Lin Mingli/painting

14. Meditation

* Dr.Lin Mingli

How I admire you
 galloping with a smile
Like flying fish in the splashing water
Is it because of Provence
 That summer is so full of dreams
Or is it the field of love flowers on the hill
That lets me lean on while I talk to the universe

－2017.2.24

－刊台灣（海星詩刊），第 24 期，2017.06
夏季號。

15. 封仔餅

樸實而親切的古早餅
像春風般溫熱
淺嚐後
我把茶斟滿
嗯……堅持一甲子
果真傳承好味道

－2017.2.23

　　　　　　－中英譯刊美國《亞特蘭大新聞》2017.3.3.
　　　　　　圖文。

Lin MingLi/photo

15. *Sealed Aberdeen Cakes*

* Dr.Lin Mingli

Simple and intimate old cakes
Like warm spring　breeze
After having a small bite
I filled the teacup
Hmm ...　having persisted for sixty　years
It really inherited the good taste

－2017.2.23

（TRANSLATOR：DR.WILLIAM　MARR
非馬　英譯）

－中英譯刊美國《亞特蘭大新聞》2017.3.3.
圖文。

16. 致珍古德博士（Dr. Jane Goodall）

妳，聖美與愛的天使
深入高山田野，為黑猩猩請命
為保育而日以繼夜
而所有榮光已種在地球村的
每一角落，化成一首真理的詩

－2017.2.24

Lin Mingli/painting

16. To Dr. Jane Goodall

* Dr.Lin Mingli

You, angel of holy beauty and love
Go deep into the alpine meadow, pleading for the chimpanzees
Work day and night for the purpose of conservation
And all the glory has been planted at every corner
of the global village
becomes a poem of truth

－2017.2.24

（TRANSLATOR：DR.WILLIAM MARR　非馬　英譯）

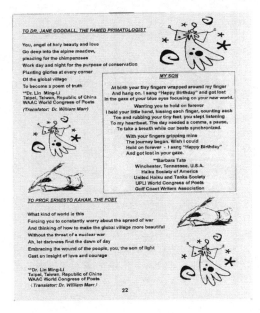

－刊美國《亞特蘭大新聞》
2017.3.10.圖文。

－英譯刊美國《世界的詩》
季刊 *Poems of The World*，
2017 年春季號，頁 22.

17. 白冷圳之戀

你，是水圳工程的驕傲
新社的母親
悠揚的山歌
那些輕拂而過的
音和雀鳥在黃昏中回轉
我便翻山越嶺
在風中
尋找你澄碧的眼眸
尋找你熾熱不落的靈魂
及守候老家鄉的靜默

你來自大甲溪，歷經風霜和
那場震變
又重新給人安慰
新社的母親啊
你灌溉了
無數旅人與遊子的心田
如星雨般動容
在群山環抱下
水聲如琴，交錯於
時間之流與月光之中

－2017.1.3

　　*白冷圳是台灣台中市一條水圳，因 1999 年 9 月 21 日，台灣歷經大地震，使白冷圳管線受損變形。後來它又被台中縣政府就地重建。它就像是台中新社地區的母親，源源不絕地提供當地的水資源，也是台灣水利工程的驕傲。如今它已成當地人飲水思源的象徵，也成了歷史活教材。

17. Love of the Bethlehem Ditch

* Dr.Lin Mingli

You are the pride of the project
Xinshe's mother
Melodious folk songs
In the wind, the sweeping sound and flying birds
Circle in the twilight
I climb over the mountains
In the wind
To look for your sparkling eyes
To look for your warm and unfailing soul
Waiting for the tranquility of my hometown

You came from Dajia River, having experienced all kind of weather
And the earthquake
Now you serve as a source of comfort
O New Town's Mother
You irrigate
The hearts of countless travelers and wanderers
Moving as the starry rain
Surrounded by mountains
The musical sound of water, interlacing
The stream of time and the moonlight

（ Translator：Dr.William Marr 非馬 英譯）
*The Bethlehem Ditch is a water in Taichung, Taiwan.
On September 21, 1999, Taiwan suffered a major earthquake

and damaged the pipeline. Later it was Taichung county government in situ reconstruction. It is like Taichung News Agency's mother, an endless stream of local water resources, but also the pride of Taiwan's water conservancy projects. Now it has become a symbol of local people drinking water source, has become a history of living materials.

刊　2017.1.3- 刊 美 國 《 亞 特 蘭 大 新 聞 》 2017.1.6　圖 文 ，
http://www.atlantachinesenews.com/News/2017/01/01-06/B_ATL_P08.pdf
　　https://www.facebook.com/AtlantaChineseNews/　錄影片貼亞特蘭大新
聞臉書

　　－ 刊 臺 灣 《 臺 灣 時 報 》 ，　2017.1.19　圖 文 。
http://www.twtimes.com.tw/?page=news&nid=620606
　　-臺灣，民視【飛閱文學地景】節目，2017.3.20 錄影於台北市「齊東詩
舍」，2017.7.15 民視新聞首次播出。

---

*2017 年.7 月 16 日於 11:23 PM 法國名詩人 Athanase Vantchev de Thracy MAIL 及**法譯此詩**

* 2017. July 16th at 11:23 pm French poet Athanase Vantchev de Thracy MAIL and the French translation of this poem

Very nice, my dear Ming-LI !

I send you your poem in French :

17. Amour du Fossé de Bethléem

*Lin Ming-Li

Vous êtes la fierté du projet,
Mère de la Cité nouvelle,
Des chants populaires mélodieux flottent dans vent,
Des chans qui pleurent et des oiseaux qui volent
En cercle dans le crépuscule.

J'escalade les montagnes,
Sous le souffle de la brise
À la recherche de vos yeux étincelants,
À la recherche de votre âme chaude et infaillible
En attendant que la tranquillité gagne ma ville natale.

Vous venez de la rivière Dajja,
Vous avez subi toute sorte de beaux et de mauvais temps,
Vous avez connu le séisme !

Maintenant, vous êtes une source de réconfort
Ô Mère de la Cité nouvelle,
Vous irriguez les cœurs d'innombrables voyageurs et pèlerins
Qui se meuvent semblables à une pluie étoilée
Cernés par les montagnes
Sous la musique de l'eau
Qui fait s'entrelacer la marche du temps et le clair de lune.

Translated into French by Athanase Vantchev de Thracy

Paris, le 16 juillet 2017

18. 棕熊

空曠溪谷的邊緣
一隻棕熊
閒晃著，吃草
春天，歌聲輕輕掠過
雪、土壤與樹
萬物也融洽於一切靜寂
牠，慢移在岩間
回想起再也無法感受的童年
靜靜等待鮭魚返鄉時
孤獨的影像
彷彿大地的史詩

－2017.3.18

Dr.Lin ingli/painting/
棕熊/ Brown bear/
林明理 畫作

18. Brown bear

*Lin Ming-Li

At the edge of the open valley
A brown bear
Is grazing leisurely
In the spring air, the sound of a song gently passing by
Snow, soil and trees
Everything is harmonious in silence
It moves slowly between the rocks
Reminiscent of the childhood that it can no longer feel
Quietly waiting for the salmons to return
A lonely image
The epic of the earth

Translator：Dr.William Marr
非馬　英譯

－2017.3.18 作

－中英譯刊中英譯美國《亞特蘭大新聞》，2017.6.9.圖文
－山東省春芽兒童文學研究會《春芽兒童文學》雜誌，2017 年 12 月，總第 10 期，封底刊林明理詩畫（棕熊）。

19. 林田山之歌

一條舊鐵道
已不再奔馳於溪谷
當我走近
這山城
早已卸下了嘆息
而風呢喃著
林場的生命故事

註：林田山 Lintiensan，位於花蓮縣鳳林鄉的林田山林業文化園區，
曾是台灣第四大的林場，規模僅次於八仙山、阿里山及太
平山等三大林場。直到 1991 年，政府全面禁伐天然林的
政策實施後，林田山的伐木作業才正式停止下來，變成沒
落的山城。如今的林田山，那些遺留在山坡上的檜木房舍
與舊鐵道，仍散發出懷舊的氣息。在林務局及文史工作者
的努力下，已保存了豐富的文化資源並陳列在林田山林業
文物展示館內，為往昔的歷史留下了見證。

—2017.4.8
—刊臺灣《臺灣時報》台灣文學版，
2017.4.19，圖文。

19. Songs of Lintiansan

*Lin Ming-Li

An old railway
No longer runs in the valley
As I approach
This mountain city
Has already unloaded its sigh
Only the wind whispers
the forest life story

（ Translator：Dr.William Marr　非馬　英譯）

* Lintiansan, located in Lin Tian Shan Forestry
Cultural Park , Fenglin Township, Hualien County

20. 詩與白冷圳的間奏曲

當我讀您

在風中，在您熾熱的靈魂裡

以鷹之姿

留給我們無限遐想

您是我生命的溫情

是我千百次

聆聽不厭的豪邁史詩

我讀您的不朽和閃光的眼眸

從翻騰苦難的歲月

到生命中幸福的一瞬

　　*二○一七年三月二十日，應邀於民視「飛閱文學地景」採訪錄影於臺北市濟南路的齊東詩舍。導演對我表述錄影經驗的觀念：不要讓稿子裡既定的內容去框住自己的思緒。要讓心房打開，才能讓自己跟觀眾間拉進距離，讓他們看到最真實的作家旁白。在四次試鏡採訪後，終於獲得了肯定的展現。此刻，我重溫著這句話，才能明白任何一次採訪錄影的來之不易。

　　歷經集集大地震又被重建的白冷圳，迄今已走過九十年歷史。它堅毅地守護著老家鄉新社等地區的形象，令人動容。那緩緩潺潺的大甲溪，那堅毅凝視的老圳，那群峰環繞的溪谷水橋，那耀眼明澈的生命之水，在空拍下將聯成一幅動人影像，賦予旅人及遊子更多的生命力。然而，誰也不曾想到這樣美的地景，卻在東岸的我身上延續了一段難忘的經驗。才學兼優的女導演林聿唯，一次次教會了我卸下的心房、弭平緊張，扔掉我心靈的包袱。最後，（白冷圳之戀）就在導演、助理編導莊晨鴻、攝影師杜星助、燈光師及彩妝師、賴坤猷等團隊的合作下完成了採訪。人與人之間的緣就是這樣，總會不期而遇。但心底對製作團隊的那份感謝不會改變。再盼有朝一日踏上台三縣中部旅遊，圓我的白冷圳之夢！

　　－2017.3.22 寫於台東

　　　　　　　　　　前排，余玉照教授，詩人林明理及葉日松夫婦，林聿唯導演，攝影師杜星助，後排，攝影助理陳樂軒，執行製作賴坤猷，助理編導莊晨鴻及梳化師 Alan。

林明理與林聿唯導演合影於齊東詩舍

— 33 — 大海洋詩雜誌

前排，余玉照教授，林明理老師及葉日松夫婦，林聿唯導
演，攝影師杜星勛，後排，攝影助理陳樂軒，執行製作賴
坤猷，助理編導莊晨鴻及梳化師Alan。

林明理博士與林聿唯導演
合影於齊東詩舍

－刊美國《亞特蘭大新聞》，2017.3.24 及合照兩張。
－刊臺灣〈大海洋〉詩雜誌，第 95 期，2017.07.頁 32-33.及照片。

21. 致詩人——Prof. Ernesto Kahan

這是怎樣的世界
讓你時刻憂心戰火蔓延
如何讓地球村更加美麗
不受核戰威脅
啊，讓黑暗去尋找黎明的那一邊
你擁抱人民的傷口，以光明之子
投射出愛與果敢的知見

－2007.3.24

Prof.Ernesto Kahan/photo

21. To Prof. Ernesto Kahan, the Poet

*Lin Ming-Li

What kind of world is this
Forcing you to constantly worry about the spread of war
And thinking of how to make the global village more beautiful
Without the threat of a nuclear war
Ah, let darkness find the dawn of day
Embracing the wound of the people, you, the son of light
Cast an insight of love and courage

－2017.3.24

（Translator：Dr.William Marr　非馬　英譯）

－刊美國《亞特蘭大新聞》，2017.4.7，圖文。
－英譯刊美國(世界的詩)季刊(Poems of The
　World)，2017 年春季號，頁 22.
*2017 年 5 月 22 日於 1:15AM Prof. Ernesto
　Kahan Mail Ming-Li
　BRAVO!!!!!!!!!!

亞特蘭大新聞
B5　Atlanta Chinese News Friday, April 7, 2017
NO 04687
Serving Since 1992

迷人的土耳其

賴淑賢

人生旅程的紅綠燈

林榮寵

十字路口紅綠燈

林明理博士詩畫

詩抄九　Prof. Ernesto Kahan

To the poet —— Prof. Ernesto Kahan

What kind of motif is this
Soaring just to summarily worry about the
speed of sea
And shirting of love to make the global
village more beautiful
Without the chime of a nuclear war
Ah, let darkness find the throng of the
Embracing the wound of the people, you,
the son of life
Cast as temple of love and courage
* Dr William Marr *

安祺的春天

V.S.A

~ 2017. 4. 7 Ming Li

TO DR. JANE GOODALL, THE FAMED PRIMATOLOGIST

You, angel of holy beauty and love
Go deep into the alpine meadow,
pleading for the chimpanzees
Work day and night for the purpose of conservation
Planting glories at every corner
Of the global village
To become a poem of truth

**Dr. Lin Ming-Li
Taipei, Taiwan, Republic of China
WAAC World Congress of Poets

(Translator: Dr. William Marr)

MY SON

At birth your tiny fingers wrapped around my finger
And hang on. I sang "Happy Birthday" and got lost
In the gaze of your blue eyes focusing on your new world.

Wanting you to hold on forever
I held your little hand, kissing each finger, counting each
Toe and rubbing your tiny feet, you slept listening
To my heartbeat. The day needed a comma, a pause,
To take a breath while our beats synchronized.

With your fingers gripping mine
The journey began. Wish I could
Hold on forever - I sang "Happy Birthday"
And got lost in your gaze.

**Barbara Tate
Winchester, Tennessee, U.S.A.
Haiku Society of America
United Haiku and Tanka Society
UPLI World Congress of Poets
Gulf Coast Writers Association

TO PROF. ERNESTO KAHAN, THE POET

What kind of world is this
Forcing you to constantly worry about the spread of war
And thinking of how to make the global village more beautiful
Without the threat of a nuclear war
Ah, let darkness find the dawn of day
Embracing the wound of the people, you, the son of light
Cast an insight of love and courage

**Dr. Lin Ming-Li
Taipei, Taiwan, Republic of China
WAAC World Congress of Poets
（Translator: Dr. William Marr）

22

22. 致生態導演──李學主

你，駕馭光線
　　投入今生所有的熱情
豐富了山水生物
來捕捉生命的感動
在天空下的福爾摩沙
　　觸摸著熟悉的泥土
潛入水域的秘境
總是想更接近
對完美圖像的渴望
記錄曾經走過的青春

　　註.生態攝影師及導演李學主以一部短片（大甲溪）獲得 2013 年電視
　　金鐘獎評審的肯定，也得到第三次金鐘最佳攝影獎，讓臺灣櫻花鉤
　　吻鮭的美麗身影成為保育工作的正能量。其近作（回到大海的蛇）
　　短片亦入圍 2015 年第五十屆電視金鐘獎。鏡頭下，無論是櫻花鉤吻
　　鮭或海蛇等美妙畫面，均表現
　　出李導演關懷各種水中生物及
　　生態的特色，因而為詩。

　　　－2017.3.31

　　　－中英譯刊美國（亞特蘭大
　　　　新聞），2017.4.14.圖文。

Lin Mingli/painting

22. To the ecological director－Lee Xuezhu

*Lin Ming-Li

You, control the light
　　Put all of your life's passion
into the　enrichment of the biological landscape
Capture the emotion of life　under the sky
　　Touch the familiar soil of　Formosa
Dive into the waters to　explore its secret
Always want to get close
To the　desire for a perfect image
And record the youth of the past

（Translator：Dr.William Marr　非馬　英譯）

23. 憶

輕輕地揮別
因為愛會惹人淚
如果再有輪迴
會不會又回到了原點
如果沒有距離
會不會讓思念減滅
我就這樣想著
不覺又過了數千年

你是雲霧裡的月光
若隱若現，航入我視界
你是繆斯的王子，是詩的泉源
到哪裡
才能揮去那盤旋不離的身影
到哪裡
才能尋回那年相遇的瞬間

啊，夢裡的詩人
讓我由衷地呼喚
我願是藍山雀
在溪谷，在雲天
痴迷於你的神奇
飛入你沉思的窗前
雀躍地哼歌
── 讓愛長遠

──2017.4.1 作

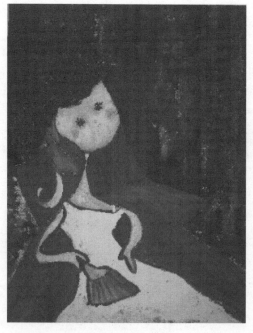

Lin Mingli/painting

23. Recollection

*Lin Ming-Li

Gently waving goodbye
For love can bring tears
If there is another reincarnation
Will it return to the origin
If there is no distance
Will it reduce longing
As I ponder
Thousands of years have slipped by

You are the moonlight in the clouds
Looming in my horizon
You are the prince of the muse, the source of poetry
Where can I go
To rid the hovering figure
Where can I go
To find the moment of encounter of that year

Ah, poet of my dream
I am sincerely calling you
Overpowered by your magic
Flies into your contemplative window
Joyfully sings
—— let our love last forever

（Translator：Dr.William Marr　非馬　英譯）

－中英譯詩畫刊美國《亞特蘭大新聞》，2017.9.1。
－中英譯刊臺灣（秋水詩刊），第 173 期，2017.10.頁 100.

24. 給 Ernesto Kahan 的祝禱

願神賜福給你，保護你
我最敬愛的朋友 Ernesto
若能插翅而飛
我願飛向你身旁
你是我心裡的支柱
──擁有巨人般的毅力
和救世的光
如今，我將時時刻刻祝禱
你的安康
為了有一天能再歡聚

註. 我的詩友 1985 年諾貝爾和平獎得主
prof.Ernesto Kahan 自今年三月罹患三叉神經
痛帶狀皰疹極其痛苦，目前已近兩個月，病
情仍不樂觀，引我擔憂不已，因而為詩。

－2017.5.3 Taiwan

－刊《臺灣時報》台灣文學版，2017.5.12.
及林明理與 Ernesto 合照。

24. Pray for Prof. Ernesto Kahan

*Lin Ming-Li

May God bless you and protect you

My most beloved friend Ernesto

If I have wings and can fly

I will fly to you

You are the pillar of my heart

With the perseverance of a giant

For your well-being

And the day of our reunion

*Note: My poetry friend, 1985 Nobel Peace Prize winner prof. Ernesto Kahan, has suffered since March of this year from trigeminal neuralgia herpes zoster which is extremely painful. And now nearly two months later, the condition is still not optimistic, which leads me to worry about him and thus write this poem.

－2017.5.3 Taiwan

（Translator：Dr.William Marr 非馬 英譯）

－刊中英譯於美國《亞特蘭大新聞》
ATLANTA CHINESE NEWS
2017.05.05. U‧S‧A，及合照。

prof.Ernesto Kahan 與林明理 Dr.Lin MingLi 於 2013 年 10 月馬來西亞舉辦的世詩會後合照。

*收件者 2017年6月19日於1:26AM PROF.ERNESTO KAHAN MAIL
My Mingli.many thanks for your emotive mails.
Today I was in Physiotherapy, after that in hydrotherapy and finally in Acupuncture. Tomorrow I will read and answer to you
love
Ernesto

25. 鵝鑾鼻燈塔

你凝視天空
恍若永恆的祈禱者
世界沉默著
你却何等剛毅——
讓巴士海峽之夜都亮了
不再畏懼七星岩暗流

飛吧，我願是鷹
嗖嗖地飛向你鼻尖前
耳畔只有潮汐起落聲
天空如明鏡無影
安閒地俯視著
所有生靈

我願在波光中
宿命地飛著
唱吧
唱出我戰鬥的幸福
請引領我
跨越黑夜，迎向光明

　　　　　　－2017.5.15 作

25. The Oluanpi Lighthouse

*Lin Ming-Li

You stare at the sky
Like an eternal prayer
The world remains silent
Yet you are so strong
The night in the Bashi Channel is so tranquil
N All creatures

I would like to fly with the waves
And sing
Sing the joy of my struggle
Please lead me
Across the night, toward the light o fear of the
undercurrents from the seven-star cave

Fly, I wish I were an eagle
Whirling around your nose and ears
Only the sound of the tide, rise and fall
The sky is as clear as a mirror
Leisurely overlooking

Translator：Dr.William Marr 非馬　英譯

－刊臺灣（青年日報）副刊，2017.6.21.
－刊大海洋詩刊）第 96 期，2018.1.頁 42

26. 吐瓦魯的悲歌

小小島國
是日漸消失的樂園
在變暖的海洋中
經歷一次次洪水和風暴

大潮來來去去
我只看見陽光哭泣
因為隨之而來的氣候難民
誰來拯救
誰能讓島民恢復生機

孤寂啊──孤寂
他們遷徙了
默默地
走向陌生的領地

註：吐瓦魯（Tuvalu）是一個由九個環形珊瑚島群組成的
　　島國，位於南太平洋。由於地勢極低，最高點僅海拔
　　四米，溫室效應造成海平面上升已對吐瓦魯造成影
　　響，是全球遭受全海平面上升威脅最嚴重的國家。國
　　際海洋學家十分憂心，如果無法有效改善地球暖化，
　　全球除了吐瓦魯以外，仍有地勢極低的國家將在數十
　　年後成為即將消失的國度，因而為詩。

　　　　　－2017.5.18
　　　　　－刊臺灣《臺灣時報》，2017.5.31，圖文。
　　　　　－中英譯刊美國《亞特蘭大新聞》，
　　　　　　2017.6.2，圖文。

26. Tuvalu's Elegy

*Lin Ming-Li

The country of small islands
Is a disappearing paradise
In the warm ocean
Endures floods and storms again and again

The tides come and go
I only see the sun weeping
Who can save the lives
Of these refugees of changing climate

Lonely - lonely
They migrate
silently
To strange and unknown territories

*International oceanographers are very worried, if global
warming is not effectively controlled, the world's low-lying
countries, in addition to Tuvalu, will all disappear within
decades.

（ Translator：Dr.William Marr 非馬 英譯）

27. 黑面琵鷺

　來自北國的
　　黑面舞者
　輕輕掠過
　　　福爾摩沙
　安靜的海岸
　或在七股灘地上佇立翻飛
　　或在魚塭中覓食
　閃光的身影
　　仿若唱歌的天使

－2017. 5.25

註. 全世界黑面琵鷺
（Black-faced spoonbill）
僅剩不到三千隻，每年來
臺灣過冬的黑面琵鷺 約
有一千多隻。牠們有時會
出現在路邊水位適當的休
耕魚塭中， 偏好夜間活
動，白天多聚集在不易遭
受干擾的海岸灘地或魚塭
休息。 臺南台江地區是
目前全世界黑面琵鷺數量
最多的棲息地。黑面琵鷺
來 台渡冬時主要在七股
潟湖、魚塭區、曾文溪口
海埔地。
－中英譯刊美國《亞特蘭
大新聞》，2017.10.27.圖文。

27. Black-faced spoonbill

*Lin Ming-Li

From the north
The black dancers
Gently slip past
　　Formosa's
Quiet coasts
Some fly or stand
On the Seven-strand land
Or search for food in fish ponds
Their flashing figures
　　Are like the singing angels

Translator：Dr.William Marr 非馬 英譯

* Note: There are less than three thousand
black-faced spoonbills around the world, about a
thousand of them come to Taiwan every winter.

28. 迷人的雕像——TO PROF.ERNESTO KAHAN

你用火般的熱情
救贖的雙手
擎起火炬，照亮世界
光輝的容顏裡
歌聲堅定
通向無數個光年

－2017.6.3

Dr.LinMingli /
painting work

28. Charming statue—TO PROF.ERNESTO KAHAN

*Lin Ming-Li

With your burning passion
And hands of salvation
You raise the torch to illuminate the world
As well as your own face
The voice of your song is firm
Lingering on for countless light years

（Translator：Dr.William Marr 非馬 英譯）

一刊美國《亞特蘭大新聞》，
2017.6.9 圖文及照片兩張。
*1985 年諾貝爾和平獎得主
ERNESTO KAHAN 於 2017 年 6
月 3 日寄來給詩人林明理的雕像
照，因而為詩畫紀念。

（ * 1985 Nobel Peace Prize
winner ERNESTO KAHAN
On June 3, 2017 sent to the poet
Lin Mingli statue, and thus
commemorate the painting and
calligraphy.）

2017.6 月 3 日於 11:34 PM Prof.
Ernesto Kahan Mail
Thanks for this superb portrait!!! Love
Ernesto

*2017 年 6 月 4 日於 3:40 PM
Prof.Ernesto Kahan Mail

My dearest Ming-Li
I'm very excited about the poem. Sees
it!!!
I'm going to put it on my Facebook
blog. Ernesto

29. 致追夢的勇士—Jennifer Bricker

一切都是可能的
這位追夢的勇士──Jennifer
為了妳的勇氣和幸福
我們將給妳更多的掌聲
讓妳的故事
交織成生命的節奏
全納入我們的心靈

*珍妮弗·布萊克（Jennifer Bricker）是美國雜技演員和空中競爭者。出生時沒有腿，她是伊利諾伊州第一個殘疾人高中挫敗的冠軍，也是作家。（寫於 2 017.6.8，Taiwan）

─中英譯刊美國《亞特蘭大新聞》，
2017.6.16 圖文。

29. *To the warrior of dreams*

* Dr.Lin Mingli

Everything is possible

To the warrior of dreams

For your courage and happiness

We will give you more applause

Let your story

Intertwine into the rhythm of life

And enter our hearts

* （Jennifer Bricker (1987) is an American acrobat and aerialist. Born without legs, she was the first handicapped high school tumbling champion in the state of Illinois and a writer.(Written on 2017.6.8, Taiwan)

（Translator：Dr.William Marr　非馬　英譯）

30. 北極熊

一隻飢餓的北極熊
躲在岸邊的雪地上
沿著海灣
徘徊在工作站旁
當牠被麻醉劑射中
救難員用直升機將牠載走
昏睡了九十分鐘後的牠
哪裡才能找到回家之路
哪裡才能找到覓食的天空

註.最近看 BBC 影片中，科學家們憂慮，因地球
冰山融化加劇，讓北極熊面臨找不到食物而
想接近人類掠取食物的悲歌。因而為詩。

－2017.6.9

30. Polar bears

*Dr.Lin Mingli

A hungry polar bear
　Hiding in the snow on the shore
Along the bay
And wandering beside a workstation
When it was shot by an anesthetic gun
And carried away by a rescue helicopter
After a ninety-minutes deep sleep
　It awakes to face the questions
Where to find the foraging space

（Translator：DR.William Marr　非馬　英譯）

*In a recent BBC film, scientists
are worried that the melting of
the iceberg of the earth is
exacerbating, so that polar bears
can not find food and want to get
close to the food of mankind.

－中英譯刊美國《亞特蘭大新
　聞》，2017.8.18 及獎狀。.

←2017.04.21 林明理博士
　獲得頒發義大利（國際閱
　讀委員會）獎狀。

31. To Giovanni Campisi

Giovanni，吾友
你從不遺忘家鄉的面貌
它是你樸實的靈魂
和自由的意志
記憶裡的食物
是意大利勞動者的智慧
在世界的每一角落裡
你告訴了我珍貴的友誼，和夢
而我以詩唱出了讚歌

*義大利詩人，（國際詩新聞）主編
Giovanni Campi si award of the Gran
Premio d'Autore.他傳電郵分享給我
此喜訊，因而為詩祝賀！

2017.6.9

Dr.Lin Mingli/painting

31. The never-forgotten love

* Dr.Lin Mingli

Dear Giovanni, my friend
You never forget the face of your hometown
It instills purity into your soul
And the will of freedom
The food of memory
Is the wisdom of the Italian laborers
At every corner of the world
You   give me precious friendship   and dream
And I praise you with my poem

（Translator：DR.William Marr
非馬 英譯）

（A poem to congratulate the
Italian poet, Giovanni Campisi,
editor of International Poetry
News, on his receiving an award
of the Gran Premio d'Autore.）

－中英譯刊美國《亞特蘭大新
聞》，2017.8.11 圖文。

32. 悼——空拍大師齊柏林

此刻，你已邁向天堂
不再憂慮了
在風雨多變的
六月——那支影片
記錄了你的光耀
也記錄了土地的滄海桑田
它深深在人民內心
被記牢。

*2017.6.10 紀錄片導演、環境保護運動者齊柏林在拍攝《看見台灣II》的空中勘景途中，於花蓮縣山區不幸墜機罹難，享年 52 歲。其代表作品《看見台灣》，曾引起社會廣大迴響，令人不捨 。-2017.6.11

Lin Mingli/Painting

32. The Master Photographer from the Air

—in memory of Mr. Qi Bolin

* Dr.Lin Mingli

At the moment, you are moving towards Heaven
Without any worry
In the unpredictable wind and rain
Of June - the film
Which recorded your glory
As well as the history of the land
Is deeply planted in the hearts
Of the people

（Translator：DR.William Marr 非馬 英譯）

* On June 10, 2017, the documentary director, an environmental protection movement activist, Mr. Qi Bolin was killed, in an airplane accident while shooting "see Taiwan II" in the mountain area of Hualien County, at the age of 52. His representative work, "See Taiwan", has made great impact on the society.

—中英譯刊美國《亞特蘭大新聞》，2017.6.16 圖文。
—刊臺灣（笠詩刊），第 320 期，2017.8，頁 106.

33. 金風鈴

你是春天的精靈
　漫在空氣裡
捎來愉悅的信息
　像是突如其來的吻
一隻蝴蝶翩翩而來
你便隨風起舞
我沒有忘記
當年回首的那一刻
　你的光芒
　　穿越黃昏的靜寂

－2017.6.13 作

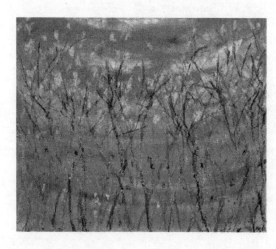

LinMingli/paint work

33. Golden Bells Forsythia

* Dr.Lin Mingli

You are the   wizard of spring
　　Diffusing in the air
Carrying   pleasant   messages
　　Like a surprise kiss
A butterfly comes dancing
You too would   dance in the wind
I have not forgotten
The moment when you glanced back that year
　　Your   brilliance
　　　　Came through the still of the evening

（Translator：Dr.William Marr 非馬 英譯）

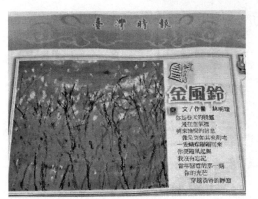

－中英譯刊美國（亞特蘭大
　新聞），2017.8.11 圖文。

－刊臺灣《臺灣時報》台灣
　文學版，2017.8.17 圖文。

－臺灣（華文現代詩），第
　　15 期，2017.11.

34.致摯友非馬 Dr.William Marr

我佇立於福爾摩沙
望穿中央山脈到大西洋
穿過海流和茂林
穿過巨石和礫灘
去追逐你奔馳的方向
我寄給你的信
是我小小的憂鬱
而你的容顏，璨爛明亮
彷彿黑暗中冉冉升起的太陽

Dr. Mingli Lin/paint

34. .William Marr

*Dr.Lin Mingli

I stand in Formosa
Looking over the central mountains toward the Atlantic Ocean
Through waves and dense forests
Through boulders and sand beaches
To follow your moving direction
My letter carries some of my melancholy
And your face, bright and brilliant
Is like the sun rising slowly from the dark

（Translator：DR.William Marr
非馬 英譯）

－2017.6.15 M.L (in Taitung)

－中英譯刊美國（亞特蘭大
新聞），2017.6.23.

35. 一則警訊

　在世界地圖上
　我看到未來
　　　繁星依舊
　一座座冰山消融
　陸地面積縮小了
　當生物面臨飢餓
　家園被毀時
　哪裡有歸路有尋
　哪裡才能避免不滅絕
　　　就這樣
　隨著大地脈搏的跳動
　　心跟著澎湃洶湧

－2017.6.13

－中英、西班牙語譯刊
　美國《亞特蘭大新聞》
　2017.7.28.圖文。

Dr.Mingli Lin /painting

35. A warning Sign

*Dr.Lin Mingli

On the world map
I see the future
The stars are still there
Except the icebergs are melting away
And the area of the land is shrinking
When the creatures are facing hunger
When the homes are being destroyed
Where to find the road of return
How to avoid extinction of all races
And so
With the beating pulse of the earth
My Heart keeps surging forth

（Translator：Dr.William Marr 非馬 英譯）

*2017.6.20. PROF. ERNESTO KAHAN
MAIL 此詩翻譯成西班牙語於 2:13
PM
This poem id great!!!!

35. Una señal de advertencia

*Dr.Lin Mingli

Observo el futuro
en un mapa del mundo...
Las estrellas siguen allí
Los icebergs se derriten lejos
y el área de la tierra se encoge.
Las criaturas enfrentan hambre
y las casas se están destruyendo.
¿Donde encontrar el camino de regreso?
¿Cómo evitar la extinción de todas las especies,
y así, con el pulso del latido de la tierra
mi corazón seguirá adelante, latiendo?

(Traducción del inglés: Ernesto Kahan)

*義大利名詩人 Giovanni　Campisi 將
此詩翻譯成義大利語 2017.8.2 於
1:04 AM MAIL Hi Ming-Li,

Your poem translated into Italian
A big hug.
Giovanni

35. UN SEGNALE DI PERICOLO

*Dr. Lin Mingli

Nella sfera di cristallo...
Vedo il futuro
Le stelle sono ancora lì
Ad eccezione degli iceberg che si sciolgono
e la superficie terrestre che si restringe.
Intanto le creature fanno la fame
e le loro case vengono distrutte.
Dove trovare la via del ritorno?
Come prevenire l'estinzione ditutte le specie?
E così
con il battito della terra
continuerà a battere, il mio cuore.

(Translation into Italian:
Giovanni Campisi)

林明理博士詩畫

1. 一則警訊

在世界地圖上
我看到未來
繁星依舊
一座座冰山消融
陸地面積縮小了
當生物面臨飢餓
家園被毀時
哪裡有歸路可尋
哪裡才能避免不滅絕
就這樣
隨著大地脈搏的跳動
心跟著澎湃洶湧
—2017.6.13

A warning Sign

* Dr.Lin Mingli

On the world map
I see the future
The stars are still there
Except the icebergs are melting away
And the area of the land is shrinking
When the creatures are facing hunger
When the homes are being destroyed
Where to find the road of return
How to avoid extinction of all races
And so
With the beating pulse of the earth
My Heart keeps surging forth
(Translator:Dr.William Marr)

*2017.6.20prof. Ernesto Kahan MAIL 將此詩翻譯成西班牙語
This poem is great!!!!
Una señal de advertencia

*Dr. Lin Mingli

Observo el futuro
en un mapa del mundo..,
Las estrellas siguen allí
Los icebergs se derriten lejos
y el área de la tierra se encoge.
Las criaturas enfrentan hambre
y las casas se están destruyendo.
¿Donde encontrar el camino de regreso?
¿Cómo evitar la extinción de todas las especies,
y así, con el pulso del latido de la tierra
mi corazón seguirá adelante, latiendo?
(Traducción del inglés: Ernesto Kahan)

2.

2.致少年的Ernesto Kahan

你滿載著夢想
穿越山川，橫渡海洋
青春的脈搏裡
沸騰著，自由而勇敢
*這位少年長大後成為醫師教授及1985年諾貝爾和平獎得主。—2017.7.20

2017.7.18ERNESTO MAIL TO MINGLI
Dearest Mingli,
I love this portrait of me when I was 15
You are great!
Ernesto
To the juvenile Ernesto

*Dr. Lin Mingli

You are full of dreams
Across the mountains and rivers
The pulse of youth
Boiling, Free and brave
* The boy grew up to become a professor of
medicine and 1985 Nobel Peace Prize winner.

3.

Mingli/Paint

3.消失的湖泊

阿特斯卡特帕湖的夜
泥水深，飢餓的小孩
讓明月低頭
滿地的空貝殼和旱地
消失的蟲鳥和生物
還有擱淺在周遭的船隻
唉，沒有收入的百姓
還能有什麼

*媒體報導，瓜地馬拉(Guatemala)西南部湖泊嚴重乾涸，百姓挨餓著，因而為詩。—2017.7.1

Disappearance of the lake

*Dr.Lin Mingli

Lake Atescatempa at night
Muddy, with hungry children
Causing the moon to lower her head
Empty shells and dry land everywhere
Disappearing insects and creatures
And there are stranded boats scattering about
Alas,without any income
What else can these people do?
* According to news report, there is severe drought in the southwestern part of Guatemala.
(Translator:Dr.William Marr)

www. AtlantaChineseNews.com P.O. Box 941070 Atlanta, GA 311

36. 諾 言

我是一粒微塵
　風的招喚，雨的垂憐
讓我飛向你
　牽動你的神經
　　觸摸你的淚腺
輕輕
吻你於額前
你會不會在深秋的雨前
　為我等候
　　或已然忘卻

－2017.6.17

Lin Mingli/pai

36. *promise*

*Dr. Lin Mingli

I am a tiny dust
　The call of the wind, the pity of the rain
Make me fly to you
　To tug at your nerves
　　Touch your lacrimal gland
lightly…
　I kiss your forehead
Will you stand in the late autumn rain
　Waiting for me
　　Or have you already forgotten

－2017.6.17

－中英譯刊美國《亞特蘭大新聞》，
2017.6.23，圖文。

37. 給最光耀的騎士
－Prof.Ernesto Kakan

你像金色的微風
在夏日裡向我走來
那悲憫的眼神裡
都是光
和愛
還有大地擁抱的
香味

注：俄羅斯貝加爾湖
〈Lake Baikal〉又稱西
伯利亞的藍眼睛，是
旅遊盛地，但今年九
月一場野火讓原本如
詩如畫的湖光山色成
了人間煉獄，有感而
文。
－2015.11.21

－刊美國《世界的詩》
《 POEMS OF THE
WORLD》，2016 年春
季號，頁 26。

37. To the most glorious knight
—Prof.Ernesto　Kakan

* Dr.Mingli Lin

You are like a golden breeze

In the summer came to me

That grievances in the eyes

Are light

And love

There is the earth to embrace

Fragrance

－2017.6.18 Taiwan

*恭喜 2017 年 4 月 6 日 Prof.Ernesto Kakan 被授予學術研究和科學查理曼的"榮譽之騎士"Knight of Honour'from Academic Institution Research　and Scientific Charlemagne on April 6 2017。特別寫此詩畫祝賀！

　　Dr.Mingli Lin Congratulations to prof.Ernesto Kahan Won the Knight of Honour'from Academic Institution Research and Scientific Charlemagne on April 6 2017. Especially to write this poetry and congratulations!

－中英譯刊美國《亞特蘭大新聞》，2017.6.30 圖文。
－刊臺灣（人間福報），副刊 2017.7.7，圖文。

*此詩創作背景：2017.6.17，Prof.Ernesto Kahan Mail to Mingli
and Mingli wrote this poem and paint for Ernesto
2017 年 6 月 17 日於 11:21 PM MAIL

Greetings from India!

I have heard from Rahul that you have been conferred 'Knight of Honour' from Academic Institution Research and Scientific Charlemagne on April 6 2017 for your outstanding contribution to the society.

Please accept my best wishes for your future endeavours.

I look forward to meeting you soon.

With Best Regards,

Ernesto

* At 2017.6.18 at 4:43 PM, Mingli immediately received Prof.Ernesto Kahan MAIL, especially moved:

Dear Mingli,

I've excited with everything you did to me,

the entire morning drawing and poems!

I already printed them, keep and if you allow me, I will put it on Facebook.

Are we friends in Facebook?

I am now going to physical therapy and take with

me these images of you and poems with the horse, which come to my heart.

I want to thank you, and I do not know how to do it.

I believe that my eyes can do it

Love

－刊臺灣（人間福報），副刊 2017.7.7，圖文。

38. 2017 年 6 月 19 日

——祝賀 Prof.Ernesto Kahan被授予"榮譽之騎士"

你的光華
像是六月的玫瑰
欣喜地
傳布
最為真摯的訊息

　　　　　　　－20176.19

Dr.LinMingli/painting

38. June 19, 2017
― congratulations Prof. Ernesto Kahan was awarded " Knight of Honour "on April 6 2017.

* Dr. Ming- li Lin

Your brilliance

Like a rose in June

Delightfully

spread

The most sincere message

―2017.6.19

―中英譯刊美國《亞特蘭大新聞》，2017.6.30 圖文。

39. 秋的懷念

秋近了，那片蘆花
　　像一隻隻飛禽出沒
槳聲和蟲鳴在黃昏的湖中回轉
　　耳邊響起的，仍是那支歌
只有風和盤旋的燕
　　混唱著。而我曳著船
在風中寫你的名字
它輕輕划過...
　　在輕揚的水面上

－2017.6.13

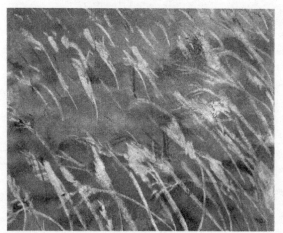

Lin Mingli/painting

39. *Memory of Autumn*

*Dr. Ming- li Lin

Autumn near, that piece of lochia

   Like a bird only infested

The oars and insects are turning in the dusk of the lake

   The ears sounded, or that song

Only the wind and circling the Yan

   Singing together. And I drag the boat

Write your name in the wind

It gently crossed it ...

   On the surface of the light Yang

－中英譯刊美國《亞特蘭大新聞》，2017.10.6，圖文。
－臺灣（華文現代詩），第 15 期，2017.11.

－刊臺灣（臺灣時報），
2017.10.5，圖文。

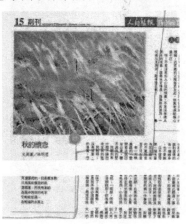

－刊臺灣（人間福報），
2017.10.11，圖文。

40. 雲 豹

牠是山林史中的精靈
沉醉於池邊的樹影
大氣和暮色
回盼來時路
尾巴溫和輕柔地擺動
　那神隱的身影
　那孤獨的靜默
被魯凱族人小心守護
在耆老們神話傳說中
　　依然存在著

—2017.6.14

*台灣雲豹(Rikulau，魯凱族語)，是魯凱族神話傳說中的祖靈，引領其祖先翻山越嶺，找到安居的樂土。目前台灣境內的雲豹已經消失，成為美麗的傳說，因而為詩。

Lin Mingli/painting

40. Rikulau

*Dr.Ming-LI Lin

It is the history of the mountains of the wizard

Immersed in the shade of the pool

Atmosphere and twilight

Back to the road

Tail gently swing gently

That divine figure

That lonely silence

Was carefully guarded by the Rukai people

In the elders of the myths and legends

Still exist

* Taiwan (Rikulau, Rukai language), is the legend of Lukai clan ancestral spirit, leading his ancestors over the mountains, to find the living paradise. At present the territory of Taiwan's clouded leopard has disappeared, become a beautiful legend, and thus for the poem.

－刊臺灣（臺灣時報），台灣文學版，2017.8.4，圖文。

－美國（亞特蘭大新聞），17.10.20，

圖文

41. 我的夢想

所有在我想像世界裡的詩
都變化於更寬廣之心的轉驛站
無論是幻想或夢境
或有多少不可能要驅馳
我相信生命是圓的
在孤獨之中仍有真正的友誼
分享彼此的快樂與苦痛

41. My dream

*Dr.Lin Mingli

All the poems in my imagination of the world
All change in the broader heart of the station
Whether it is fantasy or dream
Or how much it is impossible to drive
I believe that life is round
There is still true friendship in loneliness
Share each other's happiness and pain

-2017.6.17 morning（Translator：Dr.William
　Marr 非馬 英譯）
*收到友人 prof.Ernesto Kahan 2017.6.17Mail
　對此畫的稱讚，很開心！Received friends
　Ernesto 2017.6.17Mail praise this painting,
　very happy!
The new type of pictures, more expressionistic,
　is just great!
Ernesto-中英譯刊美國《亞特蘭大新聞》，
　2017.10.20，圖文。

42. 致 John Lennon's song – Imagine

縱使我現在還能聽見
一個滿懷和平意志與夢想的你
或許時空交會自從
我們不期而遇開始
你憂鬱的光芒
像支圓舞曲環繞整個星空
那孤獨的口哨聲
是我夢裡痛楚的溫柔

註：約翰·藍儂，MBE（John Winston Ono Lennon，出生名為 1940 年 10 月 9 日 −1980 年 12 月 8 日）是一位英國歌手和詞曲作者、披頭四樂團的創始成員，聞名全球，遇刺身亡。

Dr.Lin MIngli/painting work

42. To John Lennon's song – Imagine

*Dr. Ming-li Lin

Even if I can hear now
A peaceful will and dreams of you
Perhaps the time from time to time
We are running away from time to time
Your melancholy light
Like a round dance around the whole sky
That lonely whistle
Is my dream painful gentle

* John Lennon, MBE (John Winston Ono Lennon, born October 9, 1940 - December 8, 1980) is a founding member of the British singer and songwriter, the Beatles, the world famous, Assassination death.

－2017.6.17 作-中英譯刊美國《亞特蘭大新聞》，2017.8.11 圖文。

* 2017.6.16 MAIL 於 1:39 PM
  John Lennon is just looking!
  I admire your paint.
  You are right, I love this song, in my favorite.
  Ernesto

43. 小 象

　牠看起來這麼憂傷
　　再也不會加入家族的的歡笑
　　牠剛躲過洪水
　　卻等不到母親
回

　　　　家
　　噢！可憐的伯格

　　　　　　　　　－2017.6.20

LinMingli
/painting
work

43. The Little Elephant

*Dr.Mingli Lin

He looks so sad
Will never join the joyous family again
He has just escaped from the flood
But is still waiting for the return
　of his mother
Oh! Poor Berger

（Dr.william Marr：Translator 非馬 英譯）
－中英譯刊美國《亞特蘭大新聞》，2017.8.4
及水彩畫 1 幅.

* 2017.6.20 PROF. ERNESTO KAHAN 翻譯
此詩成英詩
My dear,
I was recommended not to sit for lung time. So,
I need to be separated from my computer as
much is possible. However, your mail are
my first priority, thus, are the first I care.
I am not a super expert in English,
I think your poem is OK, I prefer this version:

43. Baby elephant

*Dr.Mingli Lin

It looks too silent!
Is far from its laughing family.
This baby escaped the flood,
without waiting for his mother...
   Back
      Family
Oh, Poor creature!

（Translator： Prof.Ernesto Kahan）

林明理詩（小象）的中英譯刊美國
《亞特蘭大新聞》，2017.8.4 及水彩畫.

44. 現代的史懷哲
―Prof.Ernesto Kakan

你的眼神
悲憫中的萬物
　都是光
　　和慈愛
而所有澄明思想
足作為奉獻的典範

　　　　　　－2017.6.20
　　　　　　*Dr.Mingli Lin

Dr.Lin Mingli/painting

44. *Modern Shi Huizhe*
─Prof.Ernesto Kakan

*Dr.Mingli Lin

Your eyes
Everything in compassion
 Are light
  And loving
And all the clarity of thought
Enough as a model of devotion

　　─中英譯刊美國《亞特蘭大新聞》，2017.6.30，圖
文。

*2017.6.21　PROF.ERNESTO　　KAHAN　MAIL　於
12:38 PM Good morning, Mingli.Receive a big huge perfumed by spring, flowers and sun.I am very impressed and grateful for you new portrait of myself and your poems. Please send to me again the file with this portrait

Love

Ernesto

45. 這一夏夜

微風吹拂
穿過溪流
　和山崗
而我興高采烈地
　跟著奔跑
還輕吻了月

　　　　　　－2017.6.23

Dr.Lin Mingli/painting work

45. This summer night

*Dr.Mingli Lin

A breeze blows

Past the streams

    And hills

I am elated

    Running along

And tenderly kissing the moon

（ Translator：Dr.William Marr　非馬　英譯）

—中英刊美國《亞特蘭大新聞》，2017.7.7
圖文。

—英詩刊美國世界詩人大會刊物（世界的
詩）（POEMS OF THE WORLD）季刊，
2017.09 夏季號，頁 20.

45. Esta noche de verano

*Dr.Mingli Lin

Una brisa sopla
más allá de las corrientes
　y colinas.
Estoy eufórica yendo por eso
y con ternura, besar la luna

（translator ：Prof.Ernesto Kahan 翻譯此詩為
西班牙語於 2017.6.23）
　　　 * 收 件 者　**2017.6.23　PROF.ERNESTO
　　KAHAN MAIL TO MINGLI 於 4:33 PM

My mingli,
This painting is fabulous. Congratulation for this
　great art.
I wish to have some of these works you did for me. I
　am so proud of you!!!!!!
With admiration
Ernesto

*2017.7.21 法國名詩人 *Athanase Vantchev de*
Thracy 翻譯此詩為法語
Dear Ming-Li,
I like very much your peinting ! So fresh, so
　poetic !
I send you the translation of your beautiful poem
Your Friend
Athanase

45. CETTE NUIT D'ETE

Légère souffle la brise,
J'enjambe le ruisseau
Et escalade
les collines,
Toute exaltée
Je cours, enivrée, le long des champs
Et embrasse tendrement la lune.

Ming-Li

Translated into French by Athanase Vantchev de Thracy

THIS SUMMER NIGHT

A breeze blows
Past the streams
　　And hills
I am elated
　　Running along
And tenderly kissing the moon

**Dr.Mingli Lin
Taipei, Taiwan, Republic of China
WAAC World Congress of Poets
　Translator: Dr.William Marr)

一刊美國（Poems of the World）世界詩人大會季刊，2017 年夏季號，2017.09.頁 20

46. 致卡法薩巴

想像中我造訪了
卡法薩巴
我一邊深情地注視
各處
一邊尋找共鳴的開始
老城欣喜地
接納我的詩篇
　　許諾我的心願
讓我在風中
在蔚藍海面上
　　寫下你的名字

2014.6.10

—2017.6.26 寫於
prof.Ernesto Kahan 在以
色列的脊椎注射治療日。

46. To Kfar Saba, Israel

*Dr.Mingli Lin

In my imagination I visited

Cafasaba

I watched with deep feeling

throughout

While looking for the beginning of

resonance

With pleasure the old town

Accepted my poems

　　　And my wish

It let me write in the wind

And on the blue sea

　　　Your name

*Written on 2017.6.26, the day when
　prof.Ernesto Kahan of Israel received
his spine injection treatment.

（Translator：Dr.William Marr 非馬 英譯）

－英詩刊美國世界詩人大會刊物（世界的詩）
（POEMS OF THE WORLD）季刊，2017.09
　夏季號，頁 16.

－中英詩刊美國《亞特蘭大新聞》，2017.7.7，圖文。

1. To Tel Aviv, Israel
——THE BIG ORANGE

The Old town
　　Like a giant
Always stands up to listen
To the rising tide of the Mediterranean
It protects the sky
　　The distant beach
　And the sunset
While I tenderly
　　facing the night
Trigger the flow of the river of life

2. To Kfar Saba , Israel

In my imagination I visited
Cafasaba
I watched with deep feeling
throughout
While looking for the beginning of reso
With pleasure the old town
Accepted my poems
　　　And my wish
It let me write in the wind
And on the blue sea
　　　Your name

**Dr.Mingli Lin
Taipei, Taiwan, Republic of China
WAAC World Congress of Poets

(Translator : Dr. William Marr)

*Written on 2017.6.26, the day when
Prof. Ernesto Kahan of Israel received
his spine injection treatment.

47. 致以色列特拉維夫——白城

那座老城
　　如巨人般
時時兀自聆聽
　　地中海的潮起潮落
並以神的步伐
　　庇護著天空
　　那海灘在遠方
　　　夕陽在遠方
而我溫柔地
　　朝向夜晚
讓生命之河開始流動

－2017.6.26

Dr.Lin
Mingli/painting work
in Taiwan
以色列　特拉維夫——
——白城
Tel Aviv, Israel—
—THE BIG
ORANGE

47. To Tel Aviv, Israel
——THE BIG ORANGE

*Dr.Mingli Lin

The Old town
　　Like a giant
Always stands up to listen
To the rising tide of the Mediterranean
It protects the sky
The distant beach
　　And the sunset
While I tenderly
　　facing the night
Trigger the flow of the river of life

（Translator：Dr.William Marr 非馬英譯）

－英詩刊美國世界詩人大會刊物(世界的詩)（POEMS OF THE WORLD）季刊，2017.09 夏季號，頁 16.
－中英譯詩刊美國《亞特蘭大新聞》，2017.7.7，圖文。

1. To Tel Aviv, Israel
——THE BIG ORANGE

The Old town
　　Like a giant
Always stands up to listen
To the rising tide of the Mediterranean
It protects the sky
　　The distant beach

　　And the sunset
While I tenderly
　　facing the night
Trigger the flow of the river of life

2. To Kfar Saba , Israel

In my imagination I visited
Cafasaba
I watched with deep feeling
throughout
While looking for the beginning of reso
With pleasure the old town
Accepted my poems

　　And my wish
It let me write in the wind
And on the blue sea
　　Your name

**Dr.Mingli Lin
Taipei, Taiwan, Republic of China
WAAC World Congress of Poets

(*Translator : Dr. William Marr*)

Written on 2017.6.26, the day when Prof. Ernesto Kahan of Israel received his spine injection treatment.

48. 山魈

那彩面皮膚
　　像是京劇臉譜
當牠吸引母猴時
──紫色臀部便更鮮豔了
在稠密的熱帶長林山中
牠選擇了自由
　　過小群生活
白天忙著果腹
　　夜晚伴星星睡覺
瞧，這奇特的生物
　　站在山崖向南看
　　到底人類在想些什麼

*山魈，mandrill，是世界上最
　大的猴，主要生活在喀麥隆
　南部、加彭、赤道幾內亞和
　剛果的熱帶雨林中。目前由
　於偷獵和棲息地的減少，山
　魈正面臨著滅絕的危險。
－2017.6.28 作
－刊臺灣《臺灣時報》，台灣
　文學版，2017.7.12.圖文。

Dr.Lin Mingli 林明理 畫作
/nainting work in Taiwan/山魈/
mandrill

48. The Male Mandrill

*Dr.Lin Mingli

That painted skin
    Is like in Peking opera
When it tries to attract a female monkey
—— its purple buttocks become more colorful
In the dense tropical forests
It chooses freedom
    And a small group life
During the day it hunts for food
    At night it sleeps with the stars
Look!　This strange creature
    Is now standing on the cliff looking south
Wondering what thoughts are generated in human mind

（Translator：Dr.William Marr　非馬　英譯）

*Mandrills are the world's largest monkeys, live mainly in the rain forests of Southern Cameroon, Gabon, Equatorial Guinea and Congo. Currently, their survival is threatened by poaching and the reduction of their forest habitats.

49. 哈特曼山斑馬

天亮了，我充滿希望
　在世界變動的人群中
我仍喜歡在陡峭的山邊
　站崗著。
聽那些風聲和花鳥
　——察看敵情的預兆！

*哈特曼山斑馬（學名：*Equus zebra hartmannae*），又名哈氏山斑馬或山斑馬哈氏亞種，是棲息在安哥拉西南部及納米比亞西部的山斑馬亞種，是一種較為珍貴的斑馬群種，被國際自然保護聯盟（IUCN）列為易危物種。

Dr.Lin
Mingli/Painting
work in Taiwan/
哈特曼山斑馬

49. *Equus zebra hartmannae*

Dr.Mingli Lin

At dawn, I am full of hope

In the changing world

I still　like to stand guard

　At　the steep hillside

Listen to the wind and flowers and birds

　——detecting any movement of the enemy!

*outhwestern Angola and western Namibia are major habitats of Hartmann mountain zebra (scientific name: Equus zebra hartmannae), also known as Hastelloy zebra or mountain Zebra's subspecies. These zebras have become vulnerable species according to the International Union for the Conservation of Nature (IUCN).

（Translator：Dr.William Marr 非馬 英譯）

－2017.7.1 作

－刊臺灣《臺灣時報》，2017.7.5，圖文。

50. 消失的湖泊

阿特斯卡騰帕湖的夜
泥水窪，飢餓的小孩
讓明月低頭
滿地的空貝殼和旱地
消失的蟲鳥和生物
還有湖邊遍布擱淺的船隻
唉，沒有收入的百姓
還能有什麼

* 媒體報導，瓜地馬拉
(Guatemala) 西南部湖泊
嚴重乾涸，百姓挨餓著，因而
為詩。
-2017.7.1

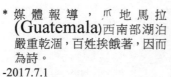

Dr.Lin Mingli/Painting work in Taiwan/
消失的湖泊 sappearance of the lake

50. Disappearance of the lake

*Dr.Lin Mingli

Lake Atescatempa at night

Muddy, with hungry children

Causing the moon to lower her head

Empty shells and dry land everywhere

Disappearing insects and creatures

And there are stranded boats scattering about

Alas,without any income

What else can these people do?

* According to news report, there is
severe drought in the southwestern
part of Guatemala.

（Translator：Dr.William Marr 非馬　英譯）

－中英譯刊美國《亞特蘭大新聞》2017.7.28.
圖文。

51.梅花鹿

別用深情的雙眸
　注視我
小溪的水聲中
我們分享著細語和
同一夢想
我們分享著牧草和
鹿仔樹苗
邊馳騁，邊聆聽大地的音調

*台灣梅花鹿（學名：*Cervus nippon taiouanus*，英文名：Formosan sika deer），為台灣特有亞種。其野外族群已在 1969 年左右滅絕，目前墾丁國家公園及綠島的野 生族群來自人工復育野放。
－2017.7.5 作

Dr.Mingli Lin/ painting
work in Taiwan 梅花鹿/
Sika deer/林明理畫作

51. Sika deer

*Dr. Mingli Lin

Do not Look at me
　With your affectionate eyes
In the sound of the stream
We share the whispers and
The same dream
We share the grass and
Deer seedlings
Together we gallop
While listening to the earth's tone

（Translator： Dr.William Marr 非馬 英譯）

*Taiwanese deer (scientific name: Cervus nippon taiouanus, English name: Formosan sika deer), is a Taiwan-specific subspecy.Its wild ethnic groups have been in extinction since1969. The current wild population in Kenting National Park and Green Island are from artificial breeding field.

－2017.7.5 作
－中英譯美國《亞特蘭大新聞》，2017.7.14，
　圖文。

52. 山的呢喃

噢赫莫薩
　　神的最深顧盼
如天使的一滴淚
　　　滴落地面般
我是一個守護者
　　　在閃耀的天地之間
聆聽樹林交響
而你靜靜晃動的眼神
既深且藍
　　　不曾改變模樣

－2017.7.8 作

Dr.Mingli Lin/painting work in
Taiwan /林明理 畫作 Hermosa

52. Mountain 's Whisper

*Dr. Mingli Lin

Oh Hermosa
God's deepest concern
Like an angel's teardrop
falling on the ground
I am a guardian
Between the shining heaven and earth
Listening to the symphony of the woods
And you just silently roll your eyes
Deep and blue
Without changing your appearance

－中英譯刊美國《亞特蘭大新聞》，
2017.7.14，圖文。

*2017.7.8 Prof.Ernesto Kahan Mail
Wonderful and beauty poem. As you are
Yes, I am happy today
Ernesto

53. 我祈禱

披著星夜
我來到橄欖山上
用純潔眼神祈禱
主啊，讓我完成夢想
且永不失力量
讓我做個讚頌祢的歌者
不再迷失徬徨
讓我記住祢的愛
在每一曙光中充滿希望
阿門

*萬國教堂位於耶路撒冷城東部的橄欖山，毗鄰客西馬尼園，是耶穌在被捕前晚間禱告的地方。

－2017.7.4

－中英譯刊美國《亞特蘭大新聞》，2017.7.14 圖文及以色列醫師詩人 Prof. Ernesto Kahan 以英語及西班牙語翻譯林明理此詩（我祈禱）。

*Prof. Ernesto Kahan 於 2017.7.8 MAIL to Dr.Mingli Lin 此詩的英文翻譯及西班牙語。

Dr.Mingli Lin/2017.7.4 Paint work in Taiwan/林明理 畫作/以色列萬國教堂

53. I pray

*Dr. Mingli Lin

Dressed in starry night
I came to the Mount of olives
To pray with my pure eyes.
Lord, let me finish my dreams
Will never lose strength.
Let me singing "we praise you"
"That we do not forget you"
Let me remind your love
In each hopeful dawn.
Amen!

西班牙語

53. ezo

Vestida de noche estrellada
Vine al Monte de los olivos
A orar con mis ojos puros.
Señor, déjame terminar mis sueños
Y que nunca pierdan fuerza
Déjame cantante que te alabamos
Que no te olvidamos
Permítame recordar tu amor
En cada amanecer lleno de esperanza.
¡Amén!

I arrange the poem at my best and translated into Spanish too. I take your hand and pray with you my Mingli

54. 我哭，在西牆

讓我做夢吧
我哭，在西牆
那來自天空的祈禱聲
低低切切，吹遍聖殿山與河谷
我將你的愛寫在地中海的群星上
恰似水藍色的風
悄悄滑過每段歷史與愛的
縐摺之痛

*傳說第二聖殿被催毀時，有天使在西牆上
哭泣，後來只有這段 18 米的殘垣斷壁留
存下來，因而西牆又稱哭牆。

— 2017.7.9 作

-中英譯刊美國《亞特蘭大新聞》，2017.7.21.
及水彩畫。Chinese and English
translation of the United States (Atlanta
Chinese News), 2017.7.21. And
watercolor painting.

54. I cry at the West Wall

*Dr. Lin Mingli

Let me dream

I cry at the west wall

The prayer from the sky

Like a low wind, blow over the temple and the valley

I will write your love on the stars of the

Mediterranean

Just like the water-blue wind

Quietly sliding over the pain

Of every history and love

（Translator ：Dr.William Marr　非馬　英譯）

*　Legend of the second temple was
destroyed, there are angels in the western
wall to cry, and later only 18 meters of
ruins left behind, so the wall called
Wailing Wall.

*Prof.Ernesto Kahan Mail 2017. 7 月　9　日

Dear Mingli,

Beautiful poem　about the Western Wall

I will write a text, that can be used as prologue of the book, if you will agree, of course. I need 4 or 5 days for that.

In the meantime please, wait. Because it is difficult to take care of many things together

Love and respect as always

Ernesto

2017.7.21 Dr. Ming-Li Lin　poem/paint

55. 我 願

像透明的風
　像浪花的樂音
我讓大自然擁抱
　將懷念到下一世

－2017.7.30

55. I wish

*Dr.MingLi

Like a transparent wind
　Like the music of the waves
I let nature embrace
　Will miss to the next generation

－中英譯刊美國《亞特蘭大新聞》，
2017.10.6

56. 致以色列拿撒勒

我來了
　　在加利利山脈的高地之下
　　千年的回憶轉啊轉
一株古樹棲息著無數野鳥
終至大平原與天空結合
而我立於神的國度
　　用盡力量呼喚
　　　　像是獻給懸崖山的風與光
然後，閱讀古城的細細紋理
　　心，竟如此溫暖

56. To Israel Nazareth

*Dr.Lin Mingli

I'm coming
    Under the highlands of the Galilee Mountains
    Memories of the Millennium keep turning
An ancient tree nested by countless wild birds
Finally the Great Plains are combined with the sky
And I stand in the kingdom of God
    With all my might I call out
    Like the wind and light dedicated to the cliff mountain
Then, read the fine texture of the ancient city
    My heart, feels so warm

Translator：Dr.william Marr 非馬 英譯

－By 2017.7.13

－中英譯刊美國《亞特蘭大新聞》，
2017.7.21.及水彩畫。

57. 感謝您—Athanase Vantchev de Thracy

你走在星野中
目光堅韌而溫柔
手握緊權杖的形貌
一邊聆聽著藍山雀和溪流
一邊創造世界文學的至寶
我跟著你前進的足音
永不會迷失方向
你是繆斯之子
必獲至上的光耀！

Mingli/paint in Taiwan

57. Thanks to you
—Athanase Vantchev de Thracy

* Dr.Mingli Lin

You walk in the wild
Eyes firm yet gentle
Hands clench to the pole of power
Listening to the blue tits and streams
While   creating the world's treasure of literature
I follow your footsteps
Never get lost
You are the son of Muse
Will eventually gain the supreme glory!

（ Translator：Dr.William Marr 非馬　英譯 ）

－2017.7.14Taiwan

－中英譯刊美國《亞特蘭大新聞》，
2017.7.21.及水彩畫。

57. MERCI À VOUS ATHANASE VANTCHEV DE THRACY

* Dr.Mingli Lin

Vous marchez dans la nature sauvage

Le regard durement éprouvé et plein de douceur,

Vos mains serrent le sceptre

Écoutant les gazouillis des mésanges　bleues

Et les hymnes des courants

Tout en enrichissant le trésor mondial de la littérature.

Je suis de près vos pas

Pour ne jamais me perdre.

Vous êtes le fils de la Muse

Destiné à la gloire suprême!

Traslated into French by Athanase Vantchev de Thracy

*2017.7.15 法國名詩人 Athanase Vantchev de Thracy
MAIL Dr.Mingli Lin 於 1:37 AM

My dear Ming-Li,

I love this portait ! It is so expressif ! Thank you dear
for your kind friendship.
　A appreciate so deeply !

Your Friend

Athanase Vantchev de Thracy /photo

58. 夜 思

是的，我想的，是你
　　——褐色眼睛
　使我無力地，像隻雷鳥
在覆雪中靜止不動

　何處有悠揚的風
　夜何以如此深重
只有雪花會來親吻
　滾燙的胸中
　分解
　　　這愛情的激動

58. Night Thoughts

*Dr. Lin Mingli

Yes, what I think of is your
   Brown eyes
Which Make me powerless, like a thunderbird
Sitting in the snow

   Where are the melodious wind
     Why the night is so deep
Only the snowflakes comes to kiss
   The passionate chest
    And break down
        The excitement of love
        by 2017.7.15

（TRANDLATOR：DR.WILLIAM MARR 非馬 英譯）

－中英譯刊美國《亞特蘭大新
聞》，2017.8.4 及水彩畫 1 幅。

法譯

58. PENSEES NOCTURNES

*Dr.Mingli Lin

Oui, ce à quoi je pense, ce sont vos yeux bruns
Qui me rendent sans pouvoir,
comme un oiseau-tonnerre posé sur la neige
où vont et viennent les vents mélodieux ?

Pourquoi d'un noir si profond sont les nuits ?
Seuls les flocons de neige viennent embrasser
la poitrine passionnée
Et apaiser
La grande excitation amoureuse.

Translated into French by Athanase Vantchev de Thracy

*2017.7.21 法國名詩人 Athanase Vantchev de Thracy 於 11:06 PM MAIL Dr.Mingli Lin 並以法語翻譯此詩

Thank you, my dear Ming-Li ! You make me happy !!!

I translated another poem of you ! Beautiful poem !!!

Your Friend

Athanase

59. 致少年的 Ernesto Kahan

你滿載著夢想
穿越山川，橫渡海洋
青春的脈搏裡
沸騰著，自由而勇敢

*這位少年長大後成為以色列醫師詩人及促進國際和平的推動者。
-2017.7.20 作

（The young man grew up to become a physician poet and a promoter of international peace.
-2017.7.20 ）

林明理畫少年的
Ernesto Kahan
/Dr.LinMingli painting work in Taiwan

59. To the juvenile Ernesto

*Dr. Lin Mingli

You are full of dreams
Across the mountains and rivers
The pulse of youth
Boiling, Free and brave

* The boy grew up to become a physician and poet for universal peace.

←中英譯刊美國《亞特蘭大新聞》2017.7.28.，圖文。

Dearest Mingli,
I love this portrait of me when I was 15
You are great!

Ernesto/photo

60. 自由

自由
　　既非戰利品或奢侈品
它應像空氣或花香般自然
而不該讓大地為它
———流血流汗

*2017.7.22 PROF.ERNESTO KAHAN 翻
譯此詩成西班牙語於 12:04 AM
PLEASE INCLUDE THIS POEM
FREEDOM in the book
Translated into Spanish from English
Ernesto Kahan
－中英及西班牙語刊美國《亞特蘭大新
聞》，2017.8.4。

60. Libertad

Libertad

no es trofeo ni artículo de lujo

Debe ser como el aire o el aroma de las flores

Por su falta la tierra suda

Y derrama sangre

—— 2017.7.22

60. Freedom

*Dr. Lin Mingli

Freedom
is neither a trophy nor an article of luxury
It should be like air or the scent of flowers
And should not for its sake let the earth sweat
Or shed blood

（Translator：Dr.William Marr　非馬　英譯）

*2017.9.5 法國名詩人 Athanase Vantchev
de Thracy　MAIL 翻譯此詩成法語　於
5:15 PM
Good morning, dear Ming-Li,

Thank you for your message. I translated
your nice little poem "Freedom"

法譯

60. LIBERTÉ

La liberté n'est ni un trophée ni un objet de luxe,
Elle devrait être comme l'air ou le parfum des fleurs
Et ne devrait pas, pour le bien de tous,
Laisser s'abîmer la terre
Ou permettre que l'on verse du sang.

Lin Mingli
Traduit en français par Athanase Vantchev de Thracy

61. 布拉格猶太人墓園

我在福爾摩莎聽到
　一支遠方的歌
一批古老的靈魂流浪著
　由一國到另一國
　直到他們找到這個地方
　可以讓他們平靜地安息了
我輕輕地
　收集你們的淚水
　擲給月光的輝耀
並在每一墓碑上……
　　　　……外加一塊石

*老猶太公墓（Starý židovský hřbitov）位
於捷克首都布拉格，自 15 世紀初開始使
用，直至 1787 年。據估計，目前發現大
約有 12,000 個墓碑，可能有多達 10 萬
人的墓葬。-2017.7.24 作

－英詩刊美國世界詩人大會刊物（世界的
詩）（POEMS OF THE WORLD）季刊，
2017.09 夏季號，頁 19.

61. The Old Jewish Cemetery in Prague

*Dr.Lin Mingli

In Formosa, I hear
　　A distant song
A group of old souls roaming
　　From one country to another
　　Until they found this place
Peaceful enough for them to settled and rest
Gently I
　　Collect your tears
　　Splash them to the glorious moonlight
And on every tombstone......
　　......　I place an extra stone

THE OLD JEWISH CEMETERY IN PRAGUE

In Formosa, I hear
　　A distant song
A group of old souls roaming
　　From one country to another
　　Until they found this place
Peaceful enough for them to settle and rest
Gently I
　　Collect your tears
Splash them to the glorious moonlight
And on every tombstone...
　　... I place an extra stone

**Dr. Lin Mingli
Taipei, Taiwan, Republic of China
WAAC World Congress of Poets

(Translator : Dr.William Marr)

*Located in the Czech capital Prague, the old Jewish Cemetery (Starý židovský hřbitov) was in use from the beginning of the 15th century until 1787. It is estimated that there are currently about 12,000 tombstones, which may have buried as many as 100,000 people.

19

（Translator：Dr.William Marr 非馬英譯）

*Located in the Czech capital Prague, the old Jewish Cemetery (Starý židovský hřbitov) was in use from the beginning of the 15th century until 1787. It is estimated that there are currently about 12,000 tombstones, which may have buried as many as 100,000 people.
—中英譯刊美國《亞特蘭大新聞》，2017.8.18

62. 戰 爭

可以肢解軀體和靈魂
可以掠奪利益和領土
　但無法沾污
詩人無聲的抗議或
　　洗去屠宰者的獸印

－2017.7.30

62. war

*Dr.Lin Mingli

It can dismember the body and spirit
It can loot the profits and the territory
But it can not contaminate
A poet's silent protest or
Wash away the tracks of the slaughtering beasts

（Translator：Dr.William Marr 非馬　英譯）

－中英譯刊美國《亞特蘭大新聞》，
2017.8.25.

－刊臺灣（文學台灣）季刊，第 104 期，
2017.10，頁 95.

63. 詩 河

你來自八荒
激勵我奇思冥想
　那叮咚的回聲
時刻盤旋著，搖曳的銀波
　輕漾藍調的柔歌

—2017.8.3

林明理 畫/ Dr. Lin Mingli Lin painting work

63. The Poetic River

*Dr. Lin Mingli

You are from a distant place
Motivate me to think
  That ding-dong echo
Ripples a blue soft song
  Over the silver waves

（Translator：Dr.William Marr　非馬　英譯）

－中英譯刊美國《亞特蘭大新聞》
2017.9.15，圖文。

64.銀背大猩猩

大地溫柔地看著
　大猩猩的影子
風與山丘寂靜……
啊，牠躲過各種侵襲
可以在森林裡睡得飽
也沒憂慮
　　——我祈禱著

*銀背大猩猩（Silverback），Gorilla Tracking）又叫金剛猩猩，是地球上現存的最大、最強壯的靈長類動物，屬於保護類野生動物。-2017.8.3

Dr.Lin Mingli /painting work in Taiwan/銀背大猩猩/ Silverback Gorilla/ 林明理 畫作

64. Silverback Gorilla

*Dr.Lin Mingli

The earth looks gently
　At the gorilla's shadow
The wind and the hills remain silent ...
Ah, after escaping from all kinds of attacks
It can now sleep soundly in the forest
Without any worry
　　——I pray

（TRANSLATOR：Dr.WILLIAM MARR　非馬英譯）

↓刊臺灣《臺灣時報》，2017.8.9.台灣文
學版，圖文。

65. 在每個山水之間

這一片憂鬱的草原啊永遠延續著
　　古老的疏林
當月亮模糊而遙遠之影
躲進了峻嶺，卻有個聲音
在每個山水之間飄蕩不停
那是鋪滿了泥草的神秘老城
在淒然的冬日
　　以蹲踞姿勢窺視
　　　　所有生物的流動之聲

我向所有的星宿裡探尋
它們深切目光使我心兒悲痛
每當冰和雪裹上了壘石的長徑
草原的歌聲便以它的柔波
　　使我在睡夢中恍惚清醒
啊那大地之詩啊已掠過微芒的東方
讓我不再佇足歎息
　　　　愛情的幻變哀音

　　－原刊臺灣（創世紀）詩雜誌，第 170 期，
　　2012.03 春季號.
　　－中英譯刊美國《亞特蘭大新聞》，
　　2017.8.25.

65. Among Hills and Rills

*Dr. Lin Mingli

The stretch of melancholy prairie is forever extending
   The ancient sparse woods
When the hazy and remote shadow of the moon
Hides in lofty mountains, there is a voice
Flowing and wafting among hills and rills
That is the mysterious old city carpeted with muddy grass
In miserable winter days
   Squatting and watching
      The running voice of all creatures

I seek and search in all the constellations
Their affectionate eyes pain my heart
Whenever ice and snow envelop the long path of stones
With soft waves the songs of prairie
   Awaken me out of my trance from sleep
     Oh poetry of the earth has flashed across the orient of dim rays of light
     For me not to stop and sigh
       At the changing sad voice of love

（現任天津師範大學，外國語系，張智中教授英譯
Professor Zhang Zhizhong English translation, Professor in Tianjin Normal University, foreign language. ）

66. 馬丘比丘之頌

我看見一隻老鷹徜徉於雲霧之中
這神廟即使是廢墟，也還是美的
加上那印弟安酋長的山巔之像
正聆聽遠方信號…它永不遺忘
來自星宿的各種訊息──從輝煌的
印加之城到現在的太陽塔日升之處

－2017.8.11 作

Dr.Mingli painting work in Taiwan/
馬丘比丘 Machu Picchu / 林明理 2017 年畫作

＊馬丘比丘 Machu Picchu 位於秘魯，是印加帝國（Incan Empire）的遺蹟。這座古城坐落於海拔 2,430 公尺的山脊上，地勢險要，有著「天空之城」及「失落的印加城市」之稱。它是世界新七大奇蹟之一，1983 年被列為世界遺產保護區。與此同時，馬丘比丘也面臨著遭旅遊業破壞的擔憂。

66. Ode to Machu Picchu

*Dr. Lin Mingli

I see an old eagle wheeling in the clouds

The temple is ruins, which is beautiful

And the statue of the Indian Chief atop the mountain

Is listening to the signal from afar … it never has lapse of memory

Various messages from the constellation — from the splendid

Incan City to the present Sun Tower where the run rises

*Machu Picchu, as the relic of the Incan Empire, is located on the mountain crest with an elevation of 2,430 meters in Peru. The terrain is strategically situated and difficult of access, hence the name of "a city in the sky" and "the lost Incan City". It is listed among the new seven wonders of the world and, in 1983 it was designated a NESCO World Heritage site. At the same time, there is worry about Machu Picchu being destroyed by tourism. — August 11, 2017

（現任天津師範大學外國語系張智中教授譯）(Translated by Prof. Zhang Zhizhong, Foreign Language Department of Tianjin Normal University)

－刊臺灣（文學台灣）季刊，第 104 期，2017.10，頁 95.

—刊臺灣（人間福報）副刊，2017.9.18，圖文。

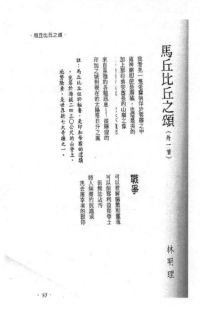

馬丘比丘之頌（外一首）

林明理

我彷彿一隻老鷹翱翔於雲霧之中
遠神廟即使是廢墟，也還是美的
加上印弟安酋長的　山巒之偉

來自星宿的各種訊息——　從瞭望的
印加之城到現在的太陽塔日升之處

戰爭

可以被解備熬和靈魂
俚輕決沾污
詩人無廢的抗議或
洗去層層苦痛的烙印

註：馬丘比丘位於祕魯，是印加帝國的遺蹟
，坐落於海拔二四三〇公尺的山脊上，
地勢險要，是世界新七大奇蹟之一。

· 馬丘比丘之頌 ·

· 95 ·

--中英譯，詩畫刊美國《亞特蘭大新聞》，亞城園地，2017.9.1。

67. 佛羅里達山獅

沿著河流拐彎處
除了風，月光，草蟲聲
　一切靜寂
牠緩慢而謹慎地
　　望向一台隱藏攝影機
然後，踮起腳尖
　　　　迅速逃離而去
這掠食者，被監視——
　　恐懼於草木之中

-2017.8.9

* 佛羅里達山獅
Florida Panther（學
名：*Puma concolor
coryi*），又名美洲
獅，牠們現存的數
量估計僅為 100 多
隻。有生態學家認
為，科學家的監視
器可能對這些掠食
者造成恐懼，促使
牠們花更多的時間
在逃跑的狀態，因
此影響進食時間也
比較少。值得關
注。

Dr.Mingli Lin painting work in Taiwan
佛羅里達山獅/ Florida Panther/ 林明理 2017 年畫作

67. Florida Panther

*Dr. Lin Mingli

Along the bend of the river
Except for winds, insect chirping, the moonshine
　Quietness reigns everywhere
Slowly and cautiously
　It looks at the hidden video camera
Then, on tiptoe
　Flees in a hurry
The predator, when overseen —
　Is startled into grass & woods

*Florida Panther (scientific name: *Puma concolor coryi*), also named puma, with estimated small number of only over 100. It is believed by some ecologists that the video camera set by the scientists may bring horror to these predators and drive them running about for life, thus influencing their diet. Attention should be paid to this.

—August 9, 2017

—（現任天津師範大學外國語系張智中教授英譯）(Translated by Prof. Zhang Zhizhong, Foreign Language Department of Tianjin Normal University)

—中英譯刊美國《亞特蘭大新聞》，2017.8.25.圖文。

68. 師恩無限

我所期待的
　九十五歲的您
——果然還是健康的模樣
豔紅的莿桐樹下
我仍是那穿著白色制服的女孩
　　由衷地默禱
風帶走我純真的歌
　　　向您行感恩之禮

*今年六月下旬在雲林縣政府文化處展覽館二樓展出莿桐國小退休的黃茂己老師父子聯展書法作品。高齡九十五歲的黃老師是我就讀國小五、六年級時期最為感念的老師，特此祝賀。
— 2017.8.8 作 - 臺灣時報，2017.10.26 圖文。

作家林明理於國小六年級時期與黃茂己老師合影於莿桐國小（Writer Lin Mingli and teacher）

68. Limitless Thanks to My Teacher

Dr. Lin Mingli

You are what I expected
At ninety five
── you still look very healthy
Under the red phoenix tree
I'm still a girl in a white uniform
Sincerely praying for the wind
To take my innocent song
My thanksgiving gift to you

（Translator：Dr.William Marr　非馬　英譯）

－刊刊臺灣《臺灣時報》，2017.10.26 台灣文
　學版，圖文。
－刊美國《亞特蘭大新聞》，2017.8.18，合照.

69. 巴巴里獅

曾經奔馳數千年
像個草原霸主
牠有清澈的灰色眼睛
　白沙似的皮膚和
　濃密的黑鬃　流蘇般
遮住了腹部...
如今，牠小憩在
納爾遜紀念碑前
安靜無聲，彷彿已然消逝　　　－2017.8.21

*巴巴里獅（*Panthera leo leo*），是世界上最大隻的獅子，也叫北非獅barbary lion，以往分布在北非，由摩洛哥至埃及，但 1922 年後最後一隻野外的巴巴里獅被射殺後，在非洲北部生存了幾千年的巴巴里獅終於在北非銷聲匿跡。現在可能只有低於 **40** 隻飼養的巴巴里獅，在動物園或馬戲團內可看見。還有，在英國倫敦的特拉法加廣場納爾遜紀念碑的獅子雕塑原型，就是巴巴里獅，也格外有雄武的風度。

Dr.Mingli Lin painting work in Taiwan Panthera leo leo/巴巴里獅 /2017 年 8 月 林明理 畫作

69. *Panthera leo leo*

*Dr.Lin Mingli

For thousands of years
It has been　lord of　the　　grassland
With clear gray eyes
　　White sandy skin and
　　Thick black mane
Covering its abdomen ...
　　Now it's resting
quietly
At the foot of Nelson Monument
As if it has already disappeared

（Translator：Dr.William Marr　非馬　英譯）

* Panthera leo leo, the world's largest　lion, also known as barbary lion, used to distribute throughout North Africa.

－中英譯刊美國《亞特蘭大新聞》 2017.9.15，圖文。

←刊臺灣《臺灣時報》，台灣文學版， 2017.9.15，圖文。

70. 義大利聖母大殿

鐘聲響了
　群鴿飛落簷上
　天空一片澄澈
這是天使與聖者的殿堂
　　我才剛踏進一會兒
陽光便細碎地灑落
　　像是給我光亮
享受片刻寧靜的時光　　　　　－2017.8.27

*聖母大殿（義大利語：Basilica di Santa Maria Maggiore）位於義大
　利羅馬，是世界上第一個以聖母命名的教堂。
－刊臺灣《臺灣時報》，台灣文學版，2017.10.19.圖文。
－中英譯刊美國《亞特蘭大新聞》，圖文，2017.10.27.
－刊義大利（國際詩新聞），圖文，中、英、義大利語翻譯及義大
　利詩人 Giovanni　Campisi 介紹林明理詩及翻譯於 2017.10.22.。

Dr.Mingli　Lin
painting　work
in Taiwan2017
年 8 月，林林
明理畫作義大
利聖母大殿
/The Temple of
Virgin Mary in
Italy

70. The Temple of Virgin Mary in Italy

*Dr.Lin Mingli

The bell rings
　　And a bevy of doves alight on the eaves
　　The sky is limpidity itself
This is the temple of angels and saints
　　Upon my stepping into it
The fine sunshine trickles and sprinkles
　　As if to give light for me
To enjoy this moment of tranquility

August, 27, 2017.

（Translator: Professor Zhang Zhizhong, Department of Foreign Languages, Tianjin Normal University，天津師範大學張智中教授英譯）

*The Temple of Virgin Mary (Italian: Basilica di Santa Maria Maggiore) is located in Rome, Italy, and it is the first church that is named after Virgin Mary.

*義大利詩人出版家 GIOVANNI　Campisi MAIL 通知其編輯的（義大利文選）書，此畫作刊封面書，此詩中文及 GIOVANNI 翻譯成義大利詩將刊於書的封底。

Giovanni2017/9/2 (週六) 12:35 AM MAIL 寫道：
Thank you so much for the Chinese original version of your poem.

I'll put your poem into Chinese and Italian on the back cover of the Poets Italian anthology that we going to prepare at this time.

On the cover we put your painting (La Basilica di Santa Maria Maggiore).

After publishing the antohology, we will send it an exemplar to Papa Francesco.

Are you agree?

Un abbraccio

Giovanni

—臺灣時報，台灣文學版，2017.10.19.圖文

*義大利 EDIZIONI UNIVERSUM（埃迪采恩尼大學）（國際詩新聞）（INTERNATIONAL POETRY　Ｎ Ｅ Ｗ Ｓ）2017.10.22 刊義大利詩人出版家 Giovanni Campisi 以義大利語翻譯林明理的中英譯詩畫（義大利聖母大殿），張智中教授英譯，Giovanni Campisi 以義大利語推介林明理此詩及翻譯如下：

義大利詩人 Giovanni Campisi 以義大利語翻譯林明理（義大利聖母大殿）詩及推介如下：

林明理，生於台灣，在國際文壇的活動散文家和詩人，是我讚賞非凡的中國藝術家和畫家；誰都喜歡畫畫的她，在其家鄉的土地美麗的地方，一直有一個特殊的吸引力於我經常在她的畫裡向我們展示了各種顏色和人物。他致力於在其母語的詩句裡翻譯，如她的這首羅馬的 Santa Maria Maggiore 聖母大殿的詩，是一個真正了不起的劇本。這是由天津師範大學外國語學院張智中教授用英文翻譯，現在由我義大利詩人約翰·坎皮西在意大利翻譯。

LIN MING-LI, POLIEDRIGA ARTISTA DI TAIWAN
CON LE SUE OPERE RENDE OMAGGIO ALL'ITALIA

Lin Ming-Li, straordinaria poliedriga artista cinese dell'isola di Taiwan, apprezzata nel panorama letterario internazionale per la sua attività di saggista e poetessa, nonché pittrice che ama dipingere i luoghi della sua meravigliosa terra natia, ha da sempre avuto una particolare attrazione per il nostro Bel Paese che spesso riproduce nei suoi dipinti di cui qui ne mostriamo uno davvero apprezzabile per la varietà dei colori e la riproduzione esatta della Basilica di Santa Maria Maggiore in Roma cui dedica la poesia nella sua madre lingua nella colonna a fianco, successivamente tradotta in lingua inglese dal professor Zhang Zhizhong del Dipartimento di lingue straniere dell'Università degli Studi di Tianjin (Taiwan) e ora tradotta dal cinese in italiano da Giovanni Campisi che qui proponiamo.

義大利語

IL TEMPIO DELLA VERGINE MARIA IN ITALIA

di **Lin Ming-Li**

Suonano le campane,

uno stormo di piccioni

vola via dalla grondaia

nel cielo azzurro

Questo è il tempio

di angeli e di santi

Sono appena arrivata

e il sole già effonde i suoi raggi

Mi piace questa luce

Mi godo questo momento

di tranquillità.

*Il Tempio della Vergine Maria (Basilica di Santa Maria Maggiore situata in Roma, Italia ed è la prima chiesa dedicata alla Vergine Maria.

Traduttore: **Giovanni Campisi**, editore, saggista, poeta e studioso delle umane cose.

71. 火車爺爺——鄧有才

他從不貪求物欲，以愛傳遞溫情。
「火車就是生命，
這是台鐵人的精神。」鄧有才說。
多年已過去，
而這故事卻歷久常新。

　　*鄧有才（1917-2010）花蓮縣民，是第一位柴油列車司機員，也是臺鐵百年經典人物，享年 94 歲，與台鐵有著七十多年深厚的感情。許多孩子都稱呼他為「火車爺爺」。-2017.8.31 作

Lin Mingli/paint

71. *Train grandfather* — Deng Youcai

*Dr.Lin Mingli

Never been a materialistic person, he loved to
deliver warmth.
"The train is my life,
This is the spirit of the Taiwanese, " said Deng.
Years have passed,
And the story is still new and fresh.

（Translator：Dr.William Marr　非馬英譯）

* Deng Youcai (1917-2010) of Hualien County,
was the first diesel train operator, and one of
the classic characters of Taiwan Railway in a
century, serving the company for over 70
years. Many children call him "train
grandfather".

－刊臺灣《臺灣時報》，台灣文學版，2017.9.7，
圖文。

－中英譯刊美國《亞特蘭大新聞》，2017.9.8，圖文。

72. 洪患

沒有人能躲過
　　那突如其來的災禍
一排排汽車
　　如玩具鴉飄浮著
大量龍捲風和強降水
　　　道路和住宅被淹沒
地球輻射平衡的變化與危害
讓人類生命，感到無所適從

　　　　　　　　　－2017.8.29

*2017 年 8 月 28 日，熱帶風暴哈維
(Harvey)已造成德州大城休士頓泡在
水中。

72. Flooding

*Dr.Lin Mingli

No one can escape
   That sudden disaster
A row of cars
   Float Like a line of toy ducks
After a large number of tornadoes and heavy rainfalls
      Roads and houses are flooded
The change of Earth's atmosphere
Has affected human life, and makes all feel at a loss

－2017.8.29

（ Translator：Dr.William Marr   非馬英譯）

* On August 28, 2017, the tropical storm
  Harvey flooded several cities in Texas,
  including Houston.

-中英譯刊美國《亞特蘭大新聞》，2017.9.8.

73. 獻給 Daniel Martini

— **Sumerian princess**

風拂過老蘆葦
　　和花芽
我想對山丘説話
對月亮的神女説話
妳的美麗與苦難
　　像詩的歌
觸及夢中不朽的國度
　　——蘇美爾

*Daniel Martini 是世上最古老的女詩
人，大祭司，也是蘇美爾公主。

－寫於 TAIWAN2017.9.4

73. To Daniel Martini
— Sumerian princess

*Dr. Lin Mingli

The wind blew over the old reeds
　　And flower buds
I want to talk to the hills
Speak to the goddess of the moon
Your beauty and suffering
　　Like a song in poetry
Touch the immortal kingdom of dreams
　　——Sumer

* Daniel Martini is the oldest poet in the
  world, the high priest, and the prince of
  Sumer.

— written in TAIWAN， 2017.9.4

－中英譯刊美國《亞特蘭大新聞》
2017.9.15，圖文。

74. 冬之歌

月光漫過草的山巔
積雪覆蓋石頭和溪流
此刻，星空覆蓋的多洛米蒂
散發純淨的光
讓我內心無比地平和

-2017.9.6

*義大利北邊多洛米蒂（The Dolomites）在
2009 年被列入世界自然遺產。

Dr.Lin Mingli /painting　/ Dolomites

74. Winter song

* Dr. Lin Mingli

Moonlight shines on the grassy mountaintop

Snow covers stones and streams

At this moment, the sky over the Dolomites

sheds pure light

Making my heart exceedingly peaceful

（Translator：Dr.William Marr 非馬 英譯）

*Dolomites, a mountain range in NE Italy,
was listed as one of the World Natural
Heritage Sites in 2009.

－中英譯刊美國《亞特蘭大新聞》，2017.10.
預稿，圖文。
－中英譯，臺灣（秋水詩刊），第 174 期，
2018.01。

75. 帕德嫩神廟

坐在巨石柱旁的大樹下
想像老城是怎樣變成今日的樣子
　　怎樣貫穿時間的秘辛
我向巨大穹蒼仰視
河水依舊不斷奔流
　　密談著愛琴海的神話故事

-by 2017.9.9

*奉祀雅典娜女神的帕德嫩神廟(The Patrhenon)是古希臘文明的重要史蹟之一，這座擁有二千五百多年歷史的城市廢墟，座落在雅典衛城（Acropolis）之巔，俯瞰著希臘首都雅典（Athens）。

—中英譯刊(美國亞特蘭大新聞)，2017.10.13，圖文。

Dr.Mingli Lin painting work in Taiwan/
The Patrhenon/帕德嫩神廟 /林明理 2017 年畫作

**義大利詩人出版家 GIOVANNI Campisi MAIL 通知其編輯的（希臘文選）書，此畫作刊其封面書。

75. The Patrhenon

*Dr.Mingli Lin

Sitting under the big tree next to the giant marble column
I Imagine how the old city has become the appearance of today
　　What is its secret of passing through time
I look up at the great sky
The river continues to run forward
　　Chatting about the myth of the Aegean Sea

（Translator：Dr.William Marr 非馬英譯）

*The **Parthenon** is a former temple on the Athenian
Acropolis, Greece, dedicated to the goddess Athena,
whom the people of Athens considered their patron.

－中英譯刊美國亞特蘭大新聞，2017.11.預稿，圖文。
－中英譯，臺灣（秋水詩刊），第 174 期，2018.01。

76. 塞哥維亞舊城

一座孤獨的城堡
　　恰似
　　　　隨風盪漾的船
　　靜靜睡在山崖上
只在夢中，回到中世紀的向晚
雲不曾改變過什麼
　　　群聚的星辰仍宴飲著
　　這一季迷人的月色

by 2017.9.11

*西班牙的塞哥維亞（Segovia）舊城，雄踞在一個狹長的山
　岩上，被列為世界文化遺產。
－中英譯刊(美國亞特蘭大新聞)，2017.10.20，圖文。

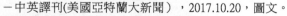

2017.9.11 Dr.Lin
Mingli painting
work in Taiwan
Segovia Castle /塞
哥維亞舊城 / 林
明理 畫作

76. The old town of Segovia

*Dr.Lin Mingli

The lone castle
  Like a boat rippling in the wind
    Sleeps quietly on the cliff
Only in a dream, it returns to the medieval evening
The cloud has not changed anything
    The stars are still feasting
  On   the charming moonlight of the season

（Translator：Dr.William Marr 非馬 英譯）

* The old town of Segovia in central
  Spain is the site of a Roman aqueduct
  and is listed as a world cultural
  heritage.

－臺灣《臺灣時報》，臺灣文學版，
  2017.11.02，圖文。
－中英譯刊美國亞特蘭大新聞，
  2017.10.20，圖文。

77. 巨石陣

來自平原的風
混雜著巨人的歎息
　　幾千年過去了
他們仍手牽手圍成大圓圈
回應著星宿的召喚
在夏至月亮升起之光裡
　　歌詠著古老的舞曲

－2017.9.14

*巨石陣 Stonehenge，是世界文化遺產，英
國威爾特郡馬平川平原上的史前建築遺
跡。我猜測可能是外星人的祭祀舞台。

Dr.Mingli Lin
painting work
巨石陣
/Stonehenge/
林明理 畫作

77. *Stonehenge*

* Dr. Lin Mingli

Wind from the plains
Carries the sigh of the giants
　Thousands of years have passed
They still hand-in-hand form a big circle
Responding to the call of the stars
In the rising moonlight of the summer solstice
　They sing together the ancient song of dance

（TRANSLATOR：　Dr.William Marr 非馬　英譯　）

* Stonehenge Stonehenge, the prehistoric monuments located on the British Wiltshire Ma Pingchuan plains, is a world's cultural heritage. In my mind, it could be a ritual stage used by the aliens.

←刊臺灣《臺灣時報》，台灣文學版，2017.9.28，圖文。

-中英譯刊美國《亞特蘭大新聞》，亞城園地版，2017.9.29，圖文。

78. 寂靜的遠山

寂靜的遠山
夜鶯，枝椏，落葉掃著水面
我以詩
　　漫射出甜美的語言
歌唱比微笑更顯著的夜空
那細微的鈴聲，隱隱傳來
　　——是牧羊人回家了

－2017.9.12

Dr.Lin Mingli painting

78. *Silence of the mountains*

*Dr. Lin Mingli

Silence of the mountains
Nightingales, branches, leaves swept the water
I have a poem
　Diffuse out of the sweet language
Singing more pronounced than the night sky
That subtle ringtones, faint came
　——is the shepherd home

（Translator：Dr.William Marr 非馬　英譯）

－中英譯刊美國《亞特蘭大新聞》，
2017.9.22.詩畫。

79. 科隆大教堂

多美的哥德式教堂！
　從東岸眺望——
上方，尖塔、星辰、灰藍
下方，河身、橋影、晃蕩
數百年過去了
它仍是西方重要的祭壇
　沉睡在星空的樂曲上

－2017.9.13

*在德國萊茵河畔的科隆大教堂 Cologne Cathedral
是世界第三高的教堂，也是世界第三大哥德式教
堂，被列名為「世界文化遺產」之一。
－中英譯刊(美國亞特蘭大新聞)，2017.10.13.圖文。

2017.9.13 Dr Lin Mingli
painting work in Taiwan 科隆
大教堂 / Cologne Cathedral
林明理 畫作.

79. Cologne Cathedral

*Dr.Lin Mingli

How beautiful is the Gothic church!
　　View from the east coast
Above, steeple, stars, and gray blue
Below, river's body and bridge's shadow are sloshing
Hundreds of years have passed
It is still an important altar of the West
　　Sleeping in the starry music

（Translator：Dr.William Marr 非馬 英譯）

* Cologne Cathedral in Cologne, Germany on the Rhine River is the third highest church in the world. It is listed as one of the "world cultural heritage".

--中譯英刊美國《亞特蘭大新聞》，2017.11.預稿，圖文.

－刊臺灣《臺灣時報》，台灣文學版，2017.10.12 圖文。

80. 金 雕

牠，飛得寂靜無聲
是唯一能直視太陽而
　　不被灼傷的神鳥
哈薩克族人如是説
數千年過去了
僅存的鷹獵人
仍騎馬跟著金雕飛馳
　　在中亞大草原上

－2017.9.17

*金雕也有人稱
為哈薩克鷹。目
前哈薩克族金
雕狩獵者僅存
約 400 人。隨著
越來越多的年
輕人遠離家鄉
外出打工，這一
傳統即將在未
來十多年後面
臨失傳危機。

Dr.Mingli Lin painting work in Taiwan 金雕/林明理 畫作

80. Golden Eagles

*Dr.Lin Mingli

They fly silently
　　And according to the Kazak people
They are the only legendary birds that dare   to
look   into the sun
Thousands of years have passed
The   surviving eagle hunters
Still ride along with the golden eagles
　　On the Prairie in Central Asia

（TRANSLATOR：　Dr.William Marr
非馬 英譯 ）

* Golden Eagles are also known as Kazakh
eagles. At present, there remain only about
400   Kazak golden eagle hunters.As more and
more young people go away from their
hometown to go out to work, the tradition is
about to face a decade of failure in the next
decade.

－中英譯刊美國《亞特蘭大新聞》，亞城園
地版，－2017.9.29，圖文。

81. 雪豹

此刻陽光照亮峰頂
雪花連翩而至
他奔向荒寒大漠
　…奔向山脊和溪谷
踩出昔日的小徑
孤獨啊
消逝在天山的盡頭
　　來去如風

　　　　　　　　　　－2017.9.25

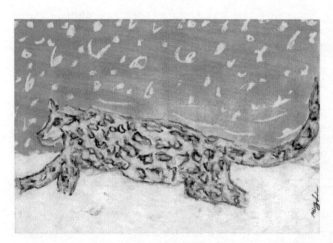

*雪豹，常在雪線附近和雪地間活動，故名「雪豹」。由於非法捕獵等多種因素，雪豹的數量正急劇減少，成為瀕危物種。天山是雪豹的聚集區之一。－中英譯刊(美國亞特蘭大新聞)，2017.10.13.圖文。

Dr.Mingli Lin painting work in Taiwan/雪豹/林明理畫作

81. *Snow Leopard*

*Dr. Lin Mingli

At this moment the sunshine illuminates the mountaintop
Snowflakes dance hither
He goes to the desolate desert
　... toward ridges and valleys
The path of yore has been trodden
Oh loneliness
Has disappeared at the end of the Heavenly Mountain
　　Coming and going like wind

*Snow leopard, whose sphere of activity is ear the snow line and the snowy land, hence its name of snow leopard. Owing to illegal hunting and other reasons, the population of snow leopards is drastically reduced, and they become an endangered species. The Heavenly Mountain is one of the gathering areas of snow leopards.

September 25, 2017（Translator：天津師範大學外國語學院 張智中教授 Translator: Professor Zhang Zhizhong, School of Foreign Languages, Tianjin Normal University）

－中英譯刊(美國亞特蘭大新聞)，2017.10.13.圖文。

82. 大貓熊

在高山陡坡的密竹林中
　周圍是一片柔和
他攀爬，翻滾奔跑
酣睡的呆萌模樣
　彷彿夢見了奇異的珍寶

—2017.10.13

*大貓熊 Giant
Panda 主要棲
息地是中國四
川、陝西和甘
肅的山區，是
中國國寶。牠
們已在地球上
生存了至少
800 萬年，被譽
為生物界的活
化石。

大貓熊 Giant Panda 林明理　畫作

82. Giant Panda

*Dr.Mingli Lin

In the steep slopes of dense bamboo forest
　　The surrounding is a soft side
He climbed and rolled
Sleep adorable look like
　　As if dream of a strange treasure

*Giant Panda's main habitat is China's
Sichuan, Shaanxi and Gansu mountain
areas, is a national treasure. They have
survived at least 8 million years on earth,
known as the living fossil of the
biological world.

－中英譯刊美國《亞特蘭大新聞》，
2017.10.27，圖文。

83. 觀白鷺

他垂下了翅羽
立於水面的岩石中
就這樣巍然不動——
彷若沉思的天使
任蜻蜓在頭上盤旋
一群野鴨款款游過
按下快門的那一瞬
我的心在雨後的校園微笑
泛著一種簡單的幸福

－2017.11.30

林明理攝影於台東大學校園

83. Observed Egret silk

* Dr.Lin Ming Li

He dropped his wings
Standing on the rock in the water
without any motion ──
Like an angel in deep thought
While dragonflies circled above his head
A group of mallard swam by
The moment I pressed the shutter
My heart smiled in the campus after the rain
Brimming with a simple happiness

(Translator：Dr.William Marr)

－中英譯刊美國《亞特蘭大新聞》，
2017.12.1，圖文。

83. Observed Egret silk

* Dr.Lin Ming Li

He dropped his wings
Standing on the rock in the water
without any motion ——
Like an angel in deep thought
While dragonflies circled above his head
A group of mallard swam by
The moment I pressed the shutter
My heart smiled in the campus after the rain
Brimming with a simple happiness

2017/12/23(週六) 5:22 PM 寫道：
My dear Ming-Li,
    I like so much your paintings and your
beautiful poem I translated into French :

83. EN OBSERVANT L'AIGRETTE NEIGEUSE

* Lin Ming Li

Elle a laissé tomber ses ailes et reste

Debout sur le rocher au milieu de l'eau

Sans le moindre mouvement –

On dirait un ange plongé dans des pensées profondes

Alors que les frêles libellules tournent autour de sa tête,

Un groupe de canards colverts passe tout près

Just au moment où j'ai appuyé sur l'obturateur.

Mon cœur a souri après la pluie

Débordant d'un simple bonheur.

Translated into French by Athanase Vantchev de Thracy

84. 在白色的森林下面

在白色的森林下面
我聽遠方細微的聲
從海峽吹來的風
　　　　默默無言地
在小徑裡面藏身
啊，我願跟著妳
放鬆片刻
讓世界保持圓型吧
　　　圓得似妳無邪的瞳孔
而我所知道的名字
就寫在今年的耶誕夜密葉上

－2017.12.12 寄給
亞城之友

亞特蘭大雪景/藍晶攝

84. *Under the white forest*

*Dr Lim Ming-li

Under the white forest
I hear the subtle voice from afar
Breeze from the Straits
                Silent
Hiding inside the trail
Ah, I will follow you
To relax for a moment
Let the world stay round
        Round as your innocent pupils
And I know the name
Written on this year's Christmas Eve leaves

（Translator：Dr.William Marr）

－刊美國《亞特蘭大新聞》，2017.12.15.
圖文。

崇高與優美的融合

──讀 Ernesto 的〈The Man and His Narrative〉

*Dr. Mingli Lin

The Blending of Sublimity and Beauty
— Reading The Man and His Narrative by Ernesto

*Dr. Mingli Lin

　　Prof. Ernesto Kahan，獲得 1985 年諾貝爾和平獎等殊榮，一位詩人型的學者。2017 年秋天，他應邀出席世界詩人大會於蒙古後，又轉往莫斯科參訪，做了一趟文化、藝術與建築之旅。之後，我便收到他遠從以色列家鄉的電郵及一首新詩創作〈The Man and His Narrative〉；反覆吟詠，給予了我多層次的審美感受。原來他的內心世界是那樣豐富！

　　Professor Ernesto Kahan, with a host of honors such as Nobel Peace Prize winner of 1985, is a scholar with something of a poet. In the autumn of 2017, after being invited to the World Poets Congress in Mongolia, he went to Moscow to experience or view the culture, art, and building there. Afterward, I received an email from him who is in his remote hometown of Israel, in which his new poem is attached: The Man and His Narrative. After reading and rereading, I have been subjected under aesthetic feelings of different hierarchies. His rich inner world surprises me!

　　這首近作是在感情催動下的生命律動，但多了些智慧和對核戰的思考。詩的內容既有形象，又有哲思；既有自然的抒情，也有優美和悲憫的情緒。既有崇高的樸素，也有堅強和精神的美。事實上，Ernesto 除了是卓越的醫師教授，也持續用他的全部思考和熱情寫著詩。而此詩的可貴處，正在於抒情中蘊聚深刻的哲思，語言具有概括力和質感，也是其心靈之聲的交響。

This new poem by him expresses the rhythm of life under inspiration, but with some wisdom and thinking about nuclear wars. The poem is with both images and philosophy, with both lyrical expression and beautiful & melancholy emotion, and with both sublime simplicity and stubborn & spiritual beauty. Actually, apart from a distinguished medical professor, Ernesto constantly devotes all his thinking and enthusiasm to poetry writing. The chief asset of this poem lies in the profound philosophy hidden in his lyricism, and his language is succinct and substantial, which contribute to the symphony of his mind.

　　總之，半個多世紀以來，Ernesto 為當代國際詩壇留下了不可抹滅的功績與成就，他是推動世界和平的舵手，在詩中渴望世界和平、愛與尊重的藝術化表現。他的行動也體現了身為和平的使者的悲憫及堅強的意志。對我而言，能分享他的新詩創作，是一大榮幸。

In short, in the past five decades, professor Ernesto has made indelible contribution to the contemporary international poetry forum. He is the promoter of world peace and in his poems, he yearns for the artistic expression of world peace, love, and respect. His action also embodies his sympathy and strong will as the messenger of peace. For me, it is a great honor to share and appreciate his new poem.

————2017.11.9 寫於臺灣

— November 9, 2017. Taiwan

The man and his narrative

By Ernesto Kahan © September 2017

男人及其敘述

歐內斯托·卡亨　　© 2017 年 9 月

You and I
on Planet Earth
walking on the steppes
and on the mud.

你和我
在地球之上
走在大草原上
走在泥土上。

On the stones and the sand,
on the grass
telling the history
of a love poem
called Adam and Eve.

在石頭和沙子之上，
在草地上
講述著亞當和夏娃
愛之詩歌
的歷史。

With animals and flowers
in bio-interaction.

動物和花朵
生物之間的相互影響。

With water and words,

air and language,

soil and bread,

our children and books.

水和話語，

空氣和語言，

土壤和麵包，

我們的孩子和書籍。

Then, to our weakness

We invented tools:

Plasma of stone, iron and bronze,

gears, and wires of electrons...

And we dominate the atom to make war.

然後，針對我們的弱點

我們發明了工具：

石頭、鐵和銅的等離子體，

工具，和電線的電子……

我們佔據原子以發動戰爭。

Oh! And always the word and the fear...

Its prayer and orders...

噢！總是話語和恐懼……

祈禱和命令……

Then, medicine was born
Its consolation,
Compassion and care.
Of an extended Oath:
Of tolerant progress,
peace, love and respect.

然後，醫藥誕生
它的安慰，
同情和關懷。
擴展的誓言：
寬容的進步，
和平，愛，尊敬。

And in friendship, today,
I open my arms to you,
To the moon, to the stars,
And to all their poets...
To the arts, you and I, perfuming the light...

在友誼中，今天，
我張開臂膀向你，

向月亮，向星星，
向所有的詩人……
向藝術，向你，向我，在陽光中噴灑香水……

（天津師範大學，張智中教授翻譯成中文(Tianjin Normal University, Professor Zhang Zhizhong translated into Chinese)）
－2017.11.29－刊美國《亞特蘭大新聞》，2017.12.1

Haikus - Perfume of Peace ...

By Ernesto Kahan © September 2017

Compassion and life,
to impede the war.
What a similarity!

On your green grassland
my timeless perfume.
Covers you in covenant

Take the bio seeds
of the tree of life.
Water them with love, today!

In all my senses
her presence is perfumed.
Death mother, my love.

Create silences

to silence the armaments
The field is at war.

Take the Silences,
spread all of them with patience!
They are waves of love.

Human skin and talk
in mixed coupled races.
Source of live seeds!

Come now beloved
to perfume our warm skin.
Human geography.

And you, my poet,
perfume, to people who works!
Blood to be alive.

Through our books
love and peace love each other.
They were living trees

In complete silence
are military hardware.
It was a poem.

你的靜默－to Giovanni 外一首

你的靜默，
在這 Capri Leone 冬季之夜──
為我開啓了想像之門，
當歲末結束──
我想到你，悲憫的歌者，你
有如溪流，將唱出希望之歌。

Your silence－to Giovanni

Your silence,
In this Capri Leone winter night ──
As I opened the door to the imagination,
When the end of the year
I think of you, compassionate singer, you
Like a stream, will sing the song of hope.

你的詩——給喬凡尼

你的詩，感情熱烈率真，
有民謠的色調，
抒情而感人。
你毫不猶豫地
表達了最純摯的
喜悅與熱情，
讓驟降在家鄉的雪
也閃著冷冷陽光
彷彿來到一個美麗的世界

Your poem—To Giovanni

Your poem, passionate and frank,
There are folk tones,
Lyrical and moving.
You do not hesitate
Expressed the most pure
Joy and enthusiasm,
Let the snow plunge in the home
Also shining cold sun
As if to a beautiful world

　　　　　－By Dr.Lin Ming-Li 2017.11.24
　　　　　－刊美國《亞特蘭大新聞》，2017.12.1。

U.S.A

Atlanta Chinese News　Friday, December 1, 2017

B4　NO. 04721

Serving Since 1992

新年，寫封信兒給女兒

◎文／董蓓

林明理博士詩畫

1.冬之歌

《義大利之聲》文學雜誌2009年第四卷第四期刊載此詩。

1.Winter song

* Dr. Lin Mingli

Moonlight dawn on the piney serene damp
Snow clouds mute and uncute
As this moment, the air over the Ordinadore
dusk gets light
Making my heart exceedingly youthful
(*Ordinadore*, a mountain range in NE Italy, was listed as one of the World Natural Heritage Sites in 2009.) Trans. lator / Dr. William Marr)

2.你的靜默---to Giovanni

Your silence---to Giovanni

3.你的詩——給喬凡尼

Your poem——To Giovanni

—Dr. Lin Ming-Li, 2017.1.26

www.AtlantaChineseNews.com P.O. Box 941070　Atlanta, GA 31141-0070　Tel:770-458-0880　Fax:770-452-0570　E-mail:info@atlantachinesenews.com

2019.12.1 Mingli

二、2017 年詩作

2017

poems & painting works

未　譯　詩

未 譯 詩

1. 春在溟濛處

　　春天的蒼鷺，飛入我的眼眸……小舟泛在水面上，微微晃盪著。

　　極目遠眺，這系列海岸山脈的河階階崖。

　　青巒疊疊晨光下，秧田車水，好似仙境！

　　我，在岸邊踱步，自己也成了水鳥。

　　時而酣睡於夢裡小河，時而歌越於漠漠水田。

　　我，飛啊飛……飛過池上平原……飛過新武呂溪沖積扇扇端的湧泉，

　　迷醉於五彩斑斕的花海，暗藍與淡青的山色相間。

　　看吶，看那溟濛純淨的山巒，大坡池的色澤多麼幽幽閃爍！

　　而我凝神諦聽，落葉的輕顫，輕拂而過的風，還有

　　香蒲沉浸在寧靜的思索中，──在淺水的草坡

上，望著你溫暖的面容。

　　噢，恬靜的波光，多麼明澈！

　　在浮圳大觀亭，瞧著，我翩翩的，越過了原野。

　　彷彿我還甜蜜地睡著了……那翻飛的記憶中的
微笑，冉冉的落在鄉路，

　　如無聲的雲朵，掠過心頭。

　　*林明理攝影作品，Dr.Lin Mingli / Photography
　攝於台灣台東縣池上鄉 / Dr.Lin Mingli photographic
works, taken in Taiwan Taitung .

　　　　　　*題目摘自於宋代蔣捷的《虞美人·梳樓》，
　　　　　　　「絲絲楊柳絲絲雨。春在溟濛處。」
　　　　　　－刊美國《亞特蘭大新聞》，2017.4.21.
　　　　　　　圖文。

未譯 2

2. 春 語

光暈下
冬不拉的草原
蹄聲和羊群於
牛背托起的太陽

雲霞被召喚
便攜著畫捲兒
嫋嫋到山樹下

在這個瞬間
我把心愛的詩集合上
夜已退隱。而外界
失去雍容、鐘擺和激昂。

只有你，引我思念
如夢的搖藍
綿延在天山

林明理　畫作 Lin Mingli/ Painting

註：冬不拉是一種哈薩克族民間流行
　　的彈撥樂器。
－2017.3.19
－刊美國《亞特蘭大新聞》，2017.4.14
　　圖文。
－刊臺灣（人間福報），副刊，
　　2017.4.24 圖文。

未譯 3

3. 安義的春天

金花開了
老村醒著
遠方的雲呵
你思念的是什麼

千畝櫻花把鄉路呵暖了
我的腳印像雀鳥般
從遠方而來
落在春雨中
落在回憶裡
你的容貌
像灰瓦上的白鴿
在風中飛翔
溫柔的羽衣
飛在思念的閨樓
飛在嬉戲的石牌坊
飛在黎明的薄霧裡

那漫漫的歲月
留下了多少動人的故事
見證了多少悲歡的歷史
一種簡單的感覺
在此相會的一瞬

這是你坐過的戲台
是你走過的小巷
是你眺望的梅嶺
而你的回眸
總是令人心醉
啊，我懷著滿腔熱情
與你漫步古塘
這是你熟悉的地方
即使在夢中也能把它找到
瞧，這越冬的田又欣欣向榮
你的歌聲是百合的模樣
你的眼裡有月亮的溫存
你的背影
在青石板小徑
就是無數旅人的家

金花開了
老村醒著
遠方的雲呵
是我思念的孤獨

－2017.3.18

Dr.Lin Mingli painting

註.安義縣在江西省，是南昌市所轄的一個縣。
－刊美國《亞特蘭大新聞》，2017.4.7.圖文。

末譯 4

4. 在風中，寫你的名字

在風中，寫你的名字，像新月一樣
當它升到山巔同白晝擦身而過，
四周是歌聲，鳥語與花香的喜悅
而你是永恆，抹不掉燈火輝煌的故鄉。

－刊美國《亞特蘭大新聞》，
圖文，2017.4.21。

Lin Mingli/painting

未譯 5

5. 幸福的火龍果

在美農村的高台間，視界多麼寬廣！
環顧四方田野──中央山脈山腳下
一畝畝火龍果正甜蜜的生活
我歡喜，讓春日的花粉穿過我的夢
那勤奮耕作的友人
帶著一朵微笑，在蜜蜂與蝶群間穿梭
而我們在歡聚的珍貴時刻
繼續享受烴窯趣及暢飲午後的太陽
啊，在這片充滿生機的土地中
復歸自然，甚為美麗，令人神往。

-2017.4.16

Lin Mingli
painting

註.2017 年 4 月 15 日，「幸福火龍果」園主邀
　請我到台東縣卑南鄉美農村三塊厝的園區去
　田間焢窯及參觀有機火龍果等作物栽種，讓
　我體會到火龍果有抑制癡呆症發生、抗衰老
　等功效，也瞭解到有機農趙開偉夫婦為種植
　火龍果所付出的心路歷程，因而為詩。
－刊美國《亞特蘭大新聞》，2017.4.28，圖文。
－刊臺灣《臺灣時報》台灣文學版，2017.4.26，
　圖文。

未譯 6

6. 你的話語 – To Giovanni Campisi

你的話語音韻優美，
如大地亮閃的雪花，
心的蔚藍所在。
我期待，
我們語言的合唱，
變成了崇高的交流，
與最美麗的感動。

－poet of Italy Giovanni Campisi
－中英譯刊美國《亞特蘭大新
聞》，2017.4.28.

6. Your words – To Giovanni Campisi

*Dr.Lin MIngli

Your words rhyme beautiful,
Such as the earth flashing snow,
The heart of the blue.

I look forward to,

The language of our chorus,

Became a lofty exchange,

With the most beautiful touched.

7. 桃花

我經由微風的振動，
凝視妳的嬌羞欲語。

7. Peach blossom

*Dr. Mingli Lin

I am through the breeze of vibration,
Stare at your shy language.

－中英譯刊美國《亞特蘭大新聞》，
2017.4.28 圖文。

末譯 8

8. 分享喜悅

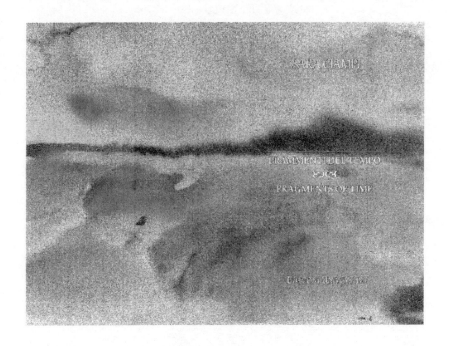

此書是女詩人 Sara Ciampi 詩集，書封面採用林明理博士的的畫，出版於義大利 2017 年 4 月。（This book is the poet Sara Ciampi poems, book cover with Dr. Lin Mingli's paintings, published in Italy in April 2017 in April.）

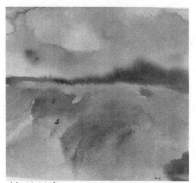

林明理畫 Dr.MingLi Lin /Paint

－中英譯刊美國《亞特蘭大新聞》，2017.4.28.

末譯 9.

9. 追悼──出版家劉振強前輩

　　你的名字
　　是臺灣出版界的豐碑
　　是萬種圖書的奠基人
　　在所有親友的追憶中
　　你，是永不枯竭的泉源
　　是文學史上永遠的財富
　　也將得到神的恩惠

　　　　　　　　　－2017.3.26

註.今年三月，文史哲出版社創辦人彭正雄先生正出版我
的新書《我的歌 My Song》時，以不捨的口吻告訴我，三
民書局創辦人劉振強先生逝世了，享年八十六歲，留給愛
戴他的員工及親友無限懷思。據瞭解，劉老先生在 2007
年曾獲新聞局主辦的第三十一屆金鼎獎「特別貢獻獎」，
在臺灣出版界有不可抹滅的貢獻，而三民書局成立迄今出
版了一萬多種圖書，也為文學史立下一個重要的里程碑。
因而為詩紀念這位卓越的出版家。

－刊臺灣《臺灣時報》，2017.3.30，圖文。

未譯 10

10 為王漢藏師畫像

你立在亞城上
從不忘記這座花園城市的面貌
歲歲年年
山茱萸開得嬌艷美麗
每一朵花瓣都是一種盛開
溫潤了多少遊子最遙遠的夢
它殘留著你的純真
你披滿陽光的笑語

在所有深愛著你的不朽記憶裡
你生命之光，何等榮耀
如鷹之姿，奮力向天飛去
那裡我們的心時時與你常在
是的，我們的摯友
你的光，已落在我們的眸子間深藏
因為有你，我們不竭之愛為你而歌

Lin Mingli painting work

－2017.2.6。為亞城詩友藍晶之先生王
漢藏教授逝世而默禱，望節哀順變。

－刊美國《亞特蘭大新聞》，2017.2.10.
圖文。

11. 春之歌

春天，你唱著穿過了花城
那是什麼樣的仙樂
讓鳥獸都在歡欣中來到你面前
讓遍地花木草葉都有了語言
那是什麼樣的仙樂
讓我一遍又一遍四處尋覓
一心要用韻律譜寫你的神秘
以及你眼裡的溫存
那是時間鳴奏著你搖映發光的臉
還是你細細端詳塵世裡的悲
噢，春天，你毋須告別
你是夢裡的雲朵
輕微的　輕微的
拂拭每個人的傷口和淚水
你是不涸的泉源
滋潤著世界萬物
任誰也譜不出你悠遠的清音
任誰也描不出你綻開的笑意

Dr.Lin Mingli/painting work

--2017.2.18-刊臺灣（秋水詩刊），
172 期，2017.07，頁 41.

－刊美國《亞特蘭大新聞》，
2017.5.26.圖文。

末譯 12

12. 珍珠的水田

夕陽西沉，蘭陽平原煙雨依舊
過去，島嶼上沒有比這更美的景色
入秋後，沒有比這更多的候鳥前來度冬
也沒有更多的水泥厝，更便利的隧道……
為了注滿一畝畝消失中的水田
為了喚回黑面琵鷺、高蹺鴴群消逝的回聲
為了塭底再也不曾出現的雁群相遇
……我覺得，這片水田哭泣了
甚至我們的後代子孫也心疼不已
我懷念，這座城鎮曾是水鳥的樂園
如今那水田映天的活的景象
正閃著光亮，只要我們翻一翻記憶
就會發現空氣中還散發出稻穗清新的氣息

－2017.4.20

註.自雪山隧道開通後，十一年來，
帶來宜蘭觀光產業增加了效益，但
也造成青年人口外流及水田生態
數量日益減少等問題。如何讓當地
公共運輸規劃與環境永續之間取
得共識，有待各界深思。

－刊臺灣《臺灣時報》，2017.5.19
　圖文。
－刊美國《亞特蘭大新聞》，
　2017.5.19，圖文。

Dr.Lin MIngli paint

未譯 13

13. 海廢危機

哭泣吧，這海洋——日以繼夜
負載著一陣悲傷
淺灣裡，旅人追逐海浪
在最歡愉的時刻
但是，無數生物
正被垃圾壓迫，無力地呼喊
那也許是哭泣的海龜、螃蟹或魚
海鳥死於網中或海廢塑膠發出的聲響
無論在島嶼、潟湖或沙灘
何時才能喚醒人類對土地的依戀
何時才能淨化人類自私的念想
你聽，那紅樹林或濕地
在小燕鷗等水鳥呼吸的地方開始歌唱
啊請飛向世界的芬芳
讓這水色一天最美的澎湖景象
一直長存到天荒地老

－2017.4.17

註.報載，澎湖原本美麗的 368
公里海岸線，現在竟然有八
成被列為廢棄物超多的紅燈
和黃燈警示區。環保人士也
十分憂心於海廢問題，因而
為詩。

Dr.Lin Mingli / painting work

－刊臺灣《臺灣時報》台灣文學
版，2017.5.24，圖文.

14. 南關清眞寺

我呼喚你，南關清真寺。
你是中國的
小麥加，真主的聖殿。
那些神秘的思想，
多次毀而復建的
阿拉伯建築與寺院，
永恆的美。
而你靜靜等待
各族人民的智慧，
以及旅人的目光
在鏡頭前閃動。
啊夜依然濃郁──
我仰望北斗諸星。
請回應吧，在莊嚴的你跟前，
我渴望和平的白鴿悠然踱步，
永不消隱。

　　　　　　　　－2017.5.19

南關清真寺　林明理

我呼喚你，南關清真寺。
你是中國的
小麥加，真主的聖殿。
那些神秘的思想，
多次毀而復建的
阿拉伯建築與寺院，
永恆的美。
而你靜靜等待
各族人民的智慧，
以及旅人的目光

在穹頂前閃動，
何夜依然濃郁——
我仰望北斗諸星。
請回應吧，在龍展的你眼前，
我渴望和平的白鴿悠然踱步，
永不消隱。

注：有鮮明阿拉伯建築風格的
南關清真大寺，是銀川的標
誌，它在寧夏省回族人民的
心目中有很高的地位。

2017.5.19

注.有鮮明阿拉伯建築風格的南關清真大寺，是銀川的
　標誌，它在寧夏省回族人民的心目中有很高的地位。

－刊臺灣（華文現代詩），第 14 期，2017.08.刊詩（南
　關清真寺），彩色攝影 2 張牡丹水庫，林明理畫當
　封面於義大利出版彩頁，林明理獲義大利（國際閱
　讀委員會）獎狀，頁 73-74。書封面底推薦林明理專
　著法譯詩集（我的歌 My Song）。

未譯 15

15. 牡丹水庫即景

挾著天光的雲朵在壩頂停留
九重葛和美麗的橋梁
讓週遭景物都恬然自足
走過哭泣湖來吧
隨我步上這老村
望著裊裊白煙升起
凝聽排灣族的生命故事
連鳥兒都緘默了
而原古的歌聲像流水
徐徐緩緩
不經意地在我身後迴響
每當夏風吹拂時
我聽到
那水聲日夜拍打著山巒
不管站在島嶼何方
都在旅人心中長存
從黃昏的四重溪落到東源村
從煙雨中的野薑花谷到水庫
啊！這湛綠的寶石
水波蕩漾
夢一般的觸動，引我相思

－2017.4.6

Lin Mingli/painting

註.牡丹水庫是屏東最大的
水庫，集取四重溪上游
的支流：汝仍溪與牡丹
溪流域的水量而成。於
1995 年興建完成，供應
著恆春、核三廠、屏南、
墾丁國家公園等用水。
周邊為原住民部落，也
有觀光景點及特色飲
食；而哭泣湖的排灣族
語，是指水流匯集之地。

－刊臺灣《臺灣時報》，
台灣文學版，2017.6.7
圖文。
－刊臺灣（笠詩刊），319
期，2017.06.頁 144.

末譯 16

16. 給愛浪潮的詩人
——高準老師並賀《詩潮》續刊

我很了解為何你喜歡浪潮
因為它了解你的傷心
和你的苦痛
你再度挺身　做出擁抱的姿勢
為了讓自己成為一員戰士
毫不在乎日漸佝僂的身軀
也遺忘了年輪滾壓的巨疼

今夜我看到……
年近八十
勞碌大半生的您
有如從雲後浮現的一顆燦星
真想穿越雲層
將你的歌與和平之鐘
在海峽兩岸的每個角落敲響

－2016.11.6 晨

－刊臺灣《詩潮》第八集，高準主編，
詩潮社 2017.5.1 出版，頁 257。

未譯 17

17. 頌黃梅挑花

我嚮往在黃梅鎮
鄰近名寺裡的那片樂土
那兒的挑花工藝
是代代相傳的婦女作品
已發展了五百年歷史
它美得像一首抒情詩
讓我內心溢滿幸福

-2017.8.21

*收到湖北省黃梅縣文化館
鄭衛國館長寄贈一條黃梅
挑花巾及詩集,很開心。
黃梅挑花被列入中國大陸
第一批國家級非物質文化
遺產名錄的民間藝術,而
鄭衛國主編過《黃梅挑花》
的書。

－刊美國《亞特蘭大新聞》,
2017.9.8.圖文。

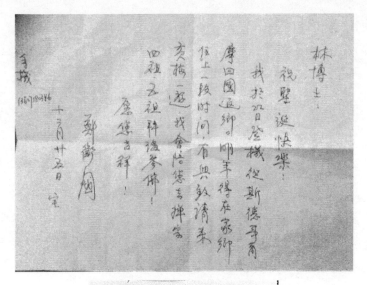

林明理博士詩畫

1.洪患

沒有人能躲過
那突襲而來的災過
一排排的生
是如冠玉魚游泳著
大量龍捲風和豪降水
洞房和住毛被淹沒
地球暖的干涉的變化與左右
陷入觀生命・感到茫然所適從

*2017年8月28日，熱帶風暴哈維
(Harvey)已造成德州大城休士頓泡在水
中。

1. Flooding

　　　　*Dr.Lin Mingli

No one can escape
That sudden disaster
A row of corn
Float Like a line of toy ducks
After a large number of tornadoes and
heavy rainfalls
　　Roads and houses are flooded
The change of Earth's atmosphere
Has affected human life, and makes all feel
at a loss
* On August 28, 2017, the tropical storm
Harvey
flooded several cities in Texas, including
Houston.

2.火車爺爺——鄧有才

花說不喜歡浪漫，以愛得歷歷過腳
「火車就是生命」
這是台灣人的精神，鄧有才說
多年已逝去
那區被稱為黑水火車爺爺

*鄧有才(1917~2018)花蓮縣民，是第一

位柴油列車可機員，也也臺灣鐵道百年經與
人物，享年94歲。與台鐵有著七十多年
深厚的感情。許多孩子都稱呼他為「火車
爺爺」。~2017.8.31

2. Train grandfather ── Deng Youcai
　　　　*Dr.Lin Mingli
Never been a materialistic person, he
loved to deliver warmth.
"The train is my life,
This is the spirit of the Taiwanese," said
Deng.
Years have passed,
And this story is still new and fresh.

* Deng Youcai (1917~2010) of Huilien
County, was the first
diesel train operator, and one of the
classic characters
of Taiwan Railway in a century, serving
the company
for over 70 years. Many children call
him "train grandfather".
(Translator: Dr. William Marr)

3.頌黃梅挑花

我常住在黃梅縣
聊過名寺裡的那片桑土
那古的挑花工藝
是代代相傳的瑰寶
它美麗動一首詩
繡我內心滿喜福

*收到湖北古美梅縣文化館筆梅縣級民
奇繡一經黃梅挑花史蹟作品・那
輕柔被列入中國大陸第一批國家級非
物質文化遺產名錄的民間發術・而那輝
固其瑰麗《紫鳳兒花》的香。~2017.8.21

2017.9.8 M.L

末譯 18.

18. 日月潭抒情

那年冬天。

我讀你的名字，Lalu。於是，蜿蜒在涵碧半島的森林氣味氤氳而來，開始有了難忘的牽掛。一葉船屋，在某些小灣上，一份閒適圍繞。

這是個充滿古老傳說的名字，在我腦海似有若無，低調、親切，泛起退思。

在月光照耀的落葉上，稀微光芒倒影的湖面，彷彿一座聖潔的水晶連橋。

每當漫步林間，偶見五色鳥、山紅頭、繡眼畫眉在隱約的樹蔭裡活潑跳躍，我便止不住內心的激動，有一種生命的喜悅經過我的身體。

我被水意和晨曦引領著。行至潭畔，眺望蔚藍色的雲朵，看白鳥剪水，看堰堤上綠草如茵。啊，Lalu，你是如此素美和富饒。

我願是展翼的歌手，聽你訴說邵族的傳說。那白色水鹿輕輕默默走過，沒有引起任何騷動，就像你生命的溫柔脈動，我只想無拘無礙在此逗留。

當明銳的陽光斜影在冬天的伊達邵碼頭，你的名字是手中的小鳥，落霞中，若隱若現……沿著堤岸在粼粼波光之上戲耍，在樹林間來回穿梭，在啁啾鳥聲中愉悅地歌咏著邵族鄉民。

　　我想站在北極星斗下採擷四季的風，讓倒映的鬱綠拴住我心深處。讓記憶裡的潭畔，穿過時空，接通了夢想。

　　我願做一尾魚，迎向起風的岸，浮雲在天上，也在湖中。而我將一種相思鑲嵌進我的詩裡，在碧波之上騰挪……

　　黎明前，朝霞像某段記憶，過濾著群山之上的風與雨。我願聆聽歲月低語，在雨後的黃昏，鑒賞雨霧繚繞的歡笑。你那朦朧的臉龐，忽而清晰起來，空氣中還存有一絲涼意。

　　你是水做的島嶼，我照見你籠在一朵朵

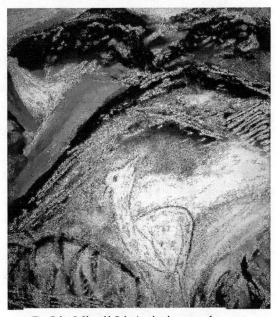

Dr.Lin Mingli Lin/painting work
*文/畫作　林明理

私密的雲海裡，可濃可淡，可墨可彩。每當落入潭中的天，藍得那麼純淨，銀波淼淼。

　　啊，Lalu，你這美麗的鳥，漸去漸遠如夢般，漫不經心地來，風中，可有我的信息？可有我為你高亢的歌？

—2016.12.9

註.拉魯島（邵語：Lalu）是一座位於南投縣日月潭中央的小島，當地居民習慣稱為珠仔山，是邵族傳說中祖靈安息之處，也有「心中聖島」之意。傳說，邵族的祖先由於打獵時發現一隻白色水鹿而沿路追逐到日月潭的拉魯島。但白鹿瞬間變成一棵白茄冬樹矗立在島上，所以邵族的祖先也從此在潭畔定居下來。因此茄冬樹成了邵族的聖樹。

—刊台灣《臺灣時報》，2017.6.22.圖文。

19. 只是一個夢

你的聲音，縈迴於我夢中
如風吹過原野
如河流過我的身邊
我毫不猶豫地
　　　　迎向你
不管夢境畢竟是虛幻的
但若是真的
我只會遠遠地望著
一動也不動...
...或許真是你在遠方呼喚著
或只是風輕輕地敲窗戲弄？

　　　　　　　　　　－2017.7.30 ML

　　　　　　　　－刊美國《亞特蘭大新聞》，2017.9.1。

20. 光耀的夜從大峪溝上升起

輝耀的夜從大峪溝上升起。

青龍山的小鎮啊，鞏義的母親！

你像一幅綠色的畫帷，南依嵩山，北靠黃河，帶給週遭百姓一片願景。

這是光伏發展的驕傲，是二十一世紀再生能源的夢土。

我們同所有的風景回來，回到這片天和使人夢想的科技園。

如今已不見數千畝荒山——只有光伏主題公園在希冀中引領中國科研創新的陸續實踐。

這兒真好：明朗，鬱鬱蔥蔥。

在未來歲月，光伏是備受矚目的科技產業。

它為綠色發展探索了新路，讓鄉民不再勞苦勞心。而溝域經濟的每一步，都使國家邁向光明。每一建設，都預知著一項嶄新的開始。

當我們從古道繞過蜿蜒的山脊，穿過慈雲寺，四山環拱，閃著一種天藍的澄淨……

在深山，在雲霧裡的禪音之間。那五十三峰像世界畫冊——罕見而莊嚴。

　　當我走向這沃土，走向叢林，走向灰瓦白牆，走向經受風風雨雨的古寺，走向聽不見淅瀝的響聲。

　　我想像，而你並不是一個傳說。我將碑刻上的故事，藏在一朵記憶的雲朵，並開始追逐這些遠山的回音。

　　勝利的老城啊！你是太陽能需求的推手——宛如魔術師。

　　從堅毅的軀體取出陽光和聖殿，再伸出手撫上我的肩頭。

　　在未來光明裡，你擎起了一份責任，為綠色世界而傲然挺立。

　　是的，就是現在。

　　當太陽從地平線上升起，我們可歌頌你的雄偉，也可移步到景景相連的密林古寺。看河水清清，看遍野的桃花林，查詢詩人杜甫故里的住處。

　　當四季的風吹過天書石，龍吟橋，還有捧月湖手搖故鄉的樂音……啊，鞏義的母親，光伏的重鎮！此刻依舊守護著子民，從不厭倦。

　　誰都無法否認。

　　只要用眼睛，就能看到你的不屈不撓。

　　只要用耳朵，就能聽見你在一個地平線把綠色能源帶進生活——既不喧囂也不矯飾的聲音！

－2017.4.3

－刊美國《亞特蘭大新聞》，2017.9.22。

21. 通海秀山行

仰臥海峽
反覆想起你的面容
那墨綠的森林睡得多香甜
從雲嶺江南間透出了
一輪明月，映照千古的詩
多光燦的穹天！

是什麼樹
把你遮得如此茂密
訴說這座雄城的蒼茫
像一首沉思的船歌

是什麼雨
和詩人一樣多情
擁有同一片天空
俯視滇中的大地

是什麼花

沿著石砌的山道
開在三元宮內
如此高雅，未曾衰老

是什麼碑刻
遍懸著歌頌你
秀甲南滇的美譽
在古柏閣的迴廊間

是什麼聲音
試圖喚起我
在純淨的光波裡
閱盡這亭臺楹聯的美妙

我泅過通海的陽光
還有古木和安詳的河流
我看見自己站在
百里杞湖，彷若隔世
而你在陽光下成長
目光炯炯，微笑如風

－刊美國《亞特蘭大新聞》，亞城園地
版，2017.9.29。

未譯 22.

22. 寫給包公故里──肥東

是怎樣的企盼，怎樣的憧憬？讓我飛越海洋的邊界，

泊在巢湖之畔，等待無比明顯的希望之城──肥東。

是的，你就像心中的巨人，堅毅而平和。

這裡美麗超出了想像，雨後大地更有麥香的味道。我懷著格外強烈的情意，再一次俯視這座石塘古鎮。

若不是從高處遠眺，怎能親近岱山的湖光山色，又怎能在風中歇息片刻，在奔向文化園路途上就有我的停留？

你說：「跟隨我吧！我是你的舵手。」

如果我往你身邊走，迎著的這股風，散發著彼處和遠方的芳菲──聽稻浪的柔音，還有那如海似的翠微。頭頂參天老木，這裡只剩下美和真。美在皖中腹地，真在耕者鋤禾裡。

輕快的白雲，群山和寧靜的沃土……都在我的血液中搏動。

溪流在岩邊跳著舞，古民也唱出心中的歌。它突破了語言的疆界，歌裡飽含著透徹的靈魂，使我

聯想起自己久別的故里，沒有任何虛妄，但我驚訝於它如何歷經千年依然為世人所傳頌？

啊，是你，使繆斯唱吟，是你震撼我的心靈，帶給勞動者心的力量。

如果我閉目靜聽，就會聽到河湖的低語，如果我凝望著那藏在山谷外的藍霧，這對我來説，彷彿是豐富的饗宴。

今夜，我依舊做著旅人的夢，夢裡用眼睛尾隨著飛逝的船隻，我感到莫名的幸福。當我目光與你對視，是你甜柔的歌聲，讓所有野花開放。

你屬於永恆，而我懷著這樣的深情，在我隱秘的心底，世上再沒有什麼樂音，讓我鼓舞地駛過萬頃波浪。

如果你看我，我就帶著江淮之間的夕陽和唇邊一朵微笑，邊哼著歡樂的小曲，駛向黑石咀的金色沙灘，在天宇間漫步，與你吟咏荷花塘。

－2016.12.6

－獲 2017 年第三屆中國包公散文獎徵文比賽 B 組散文詩三等獎，收編入中共肥東縣委宣傳部，肥東縣文聯舉辦，第三屆“中國•包公散文獎”獲獎作品集，【中國散文之鄉】，頁 287-288.

－美國《亞特蘭大新聞》，2017.10.20 刊登榮獲此詩獎作品及獎狀資訊。

*Dr.Lin Mingli won the third China in 2017
[Bao Gong essay contest]Third prize of prose.

林明理攝影於台東

292 諦 聽

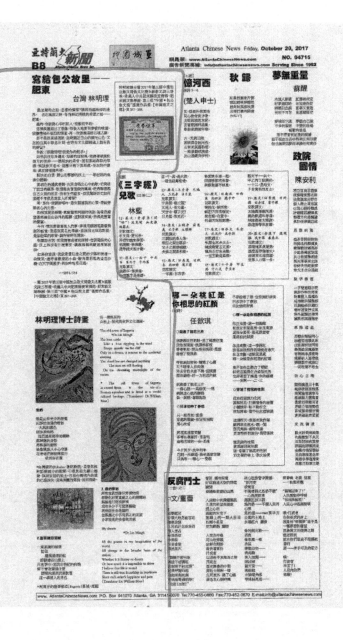

末譯 23

23. 致爾泰

但願風將思念帶去
　　只是為了你
讓我成為你的遠方
　　你唯一的知己
讓每一次偶然
　　都是久別重逢
讓我站在東岸　歌頌你

－2017.10.28 夜

胡其德教授攝影於台大農場
2017.10.26

*10 月 26 日與胡其德教授
（Robert）同遊

臺大校園，收到他寄贈的七
絕一首，有感而文。

臺大農場水塘見龜浴日　　* 胡爾泰

秋光忽破宿霾開　雲白天青入水來
偶得酥陽養頤壽　神龜靈甲上仙臺

－刊美國《亞特蘭大新聞》
2017.11.3，圖文。

24. 秋在汐止晴山

彷如重溫一個夢
　　剪剪秋風
不停地傳來潮水奔湧
一隻蝴蝶
　　　　飛上了
在瓜棚上的晴空裡
　神話一般消隱
而我聽到輕微的梵音
在山鄉的遠處
　　　　慢慢流盪
從那鮮活記憶之底層
緊緊扣著我；──啊朋友
當群星靜寂，我只求為妳而歌

2017.10.29 於台東小城

──2017.10.25，作者與葦子、余
玉照教授合影於「食養山房」。
*余與杭州詩人作家葦子溶身汐
止山水之間，一路繞峰，秋陽
杲杲。於「食養山房」入口，
接有鐵鑄橋，越樹林，復得一
水塘，錦鯉悠游眼底矣。美哉！
窗外林木鬱深，鳳蝶翩飛，綴
以美食相奉，三五蓆坐飲茗。
歸返旅程，相對忘言，唯詩音
與心靈共舞，特此以誌懷思。
──刊刊臺灣《臺灣時報》，2017.
11.10 台灣文學版，圖文。
──刊美國《亞特蘭大新聞》
2017.11.17，圖文。

未譯 25.

25. 時光裡的台大校園

*圖文 林明理

　　深秋，十點時分，天空為我們灑下光芒，傅園仍透出一份莊嚴靜謐。

　　多少次，我在這氤氳書香校園裡，開啓了閱讀之旅。

　　你在風中，微笑看著我，説：「多美的景緻！」

是啊，寬敞的椰林大道，一棟棟建築，洋溢著日式抑或現代化的剛柔相濟之美，讓我把匆忙的腳步慢下來，把心疊上農場水池的柔波裡⋯

靜在牙買加咖啡館前露天座位的大樹下。一個美麗的角落，一邊享受著翡翠檸檬汁的酸甜，一邊吟讀你的詩句。

那一刻，我愛這周遭花木扶疏，池裡的鳥、魚、烏龜、鴨、鵝，讓我的精神為之騷動，忘卻俗慮。而歡聚的時光總在驟然間悠悠而過，回到參星橫斜的月夜裡。

或者，踏青歷史，四季景致風情各異，垂柳依依。我們在傅鐘聲裡領悟人生何似的秘密。

或者，你想用手指碰觸鏡頭捕捉每一個難得的精彩瞬間。讓我的耳朵貼進你的詩思，讓花鳥的聲音與記憶東一筆西一劃地抹著湖光激灩，落英繽紛。

噢，朋友，但願在佛的庇佑下，我們能再次走訪每一條熟悉的小徑，像往常一樣，我想一直停下來，看花兒靜定地開，影印著蒼穹盡空。

讓老校長傅斯年無邊的寬厚與慈愛的光——照過來，感動著我和移動的時間都記住了醉月湖的盪漾⋯讓每一次回憶，都銘刻在心底。

—2017.11.2 寫於台東小城之夜
—刊美國《亞特蘭大新聞》2017.
12.22，圖文。

三、法國詩人 Athanase Vantchev de Thracy 翻譯成法詩

French poet Athanase Vantchev de Thracy translated into poetry

1.法國名詩人翻譯家 Athanase Vantchev de Thracy 法譯 PROF.ERNESTO KAHAN 寫序詩給林明理，祝賀林明理法譯詩集【我的歌】出版

Appendix 1.

French poet translator Athanase Vantchev de Thracy French translation of PROF.ERNESTO KAHAN write a poem to Lin Mingli, congratulations Lin Ming Li poetry translation《my song》published

Ling Ming-Li

By Ernesto Kahan © 2017

Is a poet of dreams
of light verses and
brushstrokes,
smiles and glances,
fragrance ...
Magic words and paintings
and colorful rainbows.

Oh! Beautiful poetry,
That arrive to me as light
image,
In fresh harmony,
In spring with sounds of new
flowers,
in rays of blessed light
in perfumes and songs...

Welcome life!
In paths of fantasy landscapes
ink of optimism,
rose verbs,
friendship
and love.

1985 年諾貝爾和平獎得主 Prof Ernesto Kahan 於 2017.1.10 寫詩（英語、西班牙語）贈給詩人林明理，祝賀新詩集《我的歌》出書

Ling Ming-Li
Por Ernesto Kahan © 2017

Es una poeta de sueños
de versos ligeros y pinceladas,
sonrisas y miradas,
fragancia ...
Palabras y pinturas mágicas
Y arcos iris coloridos.

Oh! Hermosa poesía,
Que me llega como imagen ligera,
En armonía fresca,
En primavera con sonidos de
flores nuevas,
En centellas de luz benditas,
En perfumes y canciones ...

Bienvenida vida!
En caminos de paisajes de fantasía
Tinta de optimismo,
Verbos color de rosa,
Amistad
y amor.

林明理

作者 Ernesto Kahan©2017

是一個夢想的詩人
是輕巧的詩和筆觸，
微笑和一瞥，
芳香...
魔詞和繪畫
以及彩虹。

哦！美麗的詩歌，
用光的圖像觸動我，
在新鮮的和諧，
在春天以新的花朵的聲音，
在受祝福的光線裡
在香水和歌曲...

歡迎生活！
在幻想風景的道路上
樂觀的墨水，
玫瑰的動詞，
友誼
和愛。

Ling Ming-Li

By Ernesto Kahan © 2017
詩人非馬英譯

*Athanase 於 2017 年 3 月 17 日於 8:40 PMMAIL
DR.LIN MINGLI

My dear Ming-Li,

Did you receive my translation into French of thepoem Mr. Kahan wrote for you ???

I send it again :

Ling Ming-Li

By Ernesto Kahan　©　2017

Is a poet of dreams
of light verses and brushstrokes,
smiles and glances,
fragrance ...
Magic words and paintings
and colorful rainbows.

Oh! Beautiful poetry,
That arrive to me as light image,
In fresh harmony,
In spring with sounds of new flowers,
in rays of blessed light
in perfumes and songs…

Welcome life!
In paths of fantasy landscapes
ink of optimism,
rose verbs,
　　　　friendship
　　　　　　and love.

IN FRENCH :

Ling Ming-Li

Est la poétesse des douces rêveries,
De vers lumineux, de gracieux coups de pinceau,
De sourires et de regards pénétrants,
De fragrance,
De style inoubliable, de peintures magiques
Et d'arcs-en-ciel pleins de couleurs.

Ô cette belle poésie
Qui m'arrive comme une image éthérée,
Poésie débordante de fraîcheur harmonieuse,
Poésie pareille à un printemps
Avec la chaude musique de ses nouvelles fleurs,
Avec ses rayons de lumière bénie,
Ses parfums et ses chansons ...

Bienvenue, ô vie,
Empruntant des sentiers
Qui traversent des paysages fantastiques !
Bienvenus encre bouillant d'optimisme,
Verbes roses,
   Amitié,
     Amour.

Thank you for thebook, dear Ming-Li !
Your Friend
Athanase Vantchev de Thracy
http://www.athanase.org

2. Athanase Vantchev de Thracy

法譯林明理二首詩作

Athanase Vantchev de Thracy Translated by Lin Mingli

法國名詩人 Athanase Vantchev de Thracy 照

1.噢，摩洛哥

*林明理

噢，摩洛哥
神秘而奇特
有古典的淡傷
有現代的魔幻
它是愛情的交響曲
是詩人讚頌的魔都

1. Oh, Morocco

*Dr.Mingli Lin

Oh, Morocco
Mysterious and peculiar
There is a classical light injury
There is a modern magic
It is the symphony of love
Is the poet praise the magic of all

法譯 FRENCH：

1. Oh, Maroc

Oh, Maroc,

Pays mystérieux, pays particulier,

Royaume blessé par l'éclat de la lumière pure,

Contrée marquée par la magie moderne !

Oh, Maroc,

Tu es une symphonie d'amour !

Poète, mon ami, fais l'éloge de tous les êtres

Qui vivent heureux sur cette terre bénie!

Ming-Li

Adapté en français par Athanase Vantchev de Thracy

*French famous poet Athanase Vantchev de Thracy

2.致訪遊中的詩人

─Athanase Vantchev de Thracy

*林明理

你高坐在殿前，似聖徒
深邃而熱烈地凝視
哦，光耀的摩洛哥
──上帝的花園，彩繪的沉思
那山歌，沙漠，峽谷
竟是你最深的眷顧！

　　　　　　　　－2017.3.23

2.Dr. Ming-Li – the poet Athanase Vantchev de Thracy – In the tour

*Dr.Mingli Lin

You sit high in front of the temple, like a saint

Deep and warmly staring

Oh, glorious Morocco

— God's garden, painted meditation

That mountain song, desert, canyon

Was your deepest care!

法譯 IN FRENCH

2.Dr. Ming-Li – Athanase Vantchev de Thracy –le poète dans sa tour

Vous vous tenez en haut devant le temple, comme un saint

Profond et le regard plein de chaleur :

Oh, glorieux Maroc

－Jardin de Dieu, méditation radieuse –

Ces chants de montagne, ces déserts, ces canyons

Étaient l' objet de votre plus grande attention !

　　　　－中、英、法譯刊美國《亞特蘭大新聞》，2017.3.31.

四、義大利名詩人 Giovanni Campisi 以義大利語贈詩給林明理詩歌 3 首

The Italian poet Giovanni Campisi gives poems to the poems of Lin Mingli in Italian

1. * **2017** 年 **8** 月 **16** 日於 1:09 AM MAIL MINGLI

Hi Ming-Li,

Many thanks for your poem, I appreciate it so much.
I write one for you into Italian now.

My poem for you

Per la mia amica Ming-Li

Amica preziosa,
davvero graziosa,
sempre sorridente,
allegra, indipendente.

Poetessa di grande valore
scrive poesie a tutte le ore
ha sempre ricca di nuove idee
ed è più bella di tutte le dee.

I'll send the translation into English, but it will be so nice
like into Italian

我的朋友－明理

我珍貴的朋友，
真的很漂亮，
總是面帶微笑，
開朗，獨立的。

很有價值的女詩人，
他的全部時間寫的詩，
總是充滿新意，
是最漂亮的女神。

2017.10.20 義大利詩人 Giovanni 於 1:09 AM mail 給 Lin Mingli 一首義大利詩

Hi Ming-Li,

I no longer have your news.
How are you?
Write me when you can.
A strong hug
Giovanni

Per la mia amica Ming-Li

Non perdo di te neppure un fiore
e tornerò a parlarti per ore.

Ci sarà nell'aria profumo di miele
se non ammainerai le vele.

Ti racconterò di come nasce il sole
prima che faccia le spole

tra Roma e Singapore.

2017 年 1 月 4 日於 2:20AMGiovannimail to Mingli a poem

Hi Ming-Li,
hereby my poem for you.
Let me know what you think about it.
A big hug.
Giovanni

THE STAR OF TAIWAN	LA STELLA DI TAIWAN
To Ming-Li	A Ming-Li
In your eyes	Nei tuoi occhi
shines the sun	splende il sole
of Taiwan	di Taiwan
In your heart	Nel tuo cuore
flourishes your love	fiorisce l' amore
for humanity	per l' umanità
In your mind	Nella tua mente
you look at the stars	cerchi le stelle
the most beautiful of universe	più belle dell' universo
And you're a woman	E sei donna
you are able to love	che sai amare
the world	il mondo
around you	che ti circonda
and also that	e anche quello
farther	più lontano
of your home.	della tua patria.

五、醫師詩人 Prof. Ernesto Kahan（獲1985年諾貝爾和平獎）2017.7.1 Mail Dr.Lin Mingli 的英詩及西班牙語詩二首

Physician poet Prof. Ernesto Kahan (won the 1985 Nobel Peace Prize) Mail Mingli's English and Spanish poems

＊1985年諾貝爾和平獎的醫師詩人 Prof. Ernesto Kahan 於 2017/7/1 PM14:57 .Mail Mingli 的英詩及西班牙語詩：

1. You are my symbol of the healthy you

Mingli,

You are my symbol of the healthy youth,

The smile that catches the day not to let they go,

Hands painting the imagined life,

A mouth pronouncing the magic words

for the beautiful and beloved human poetry.

A flower in the grass that grows happy after the rain

And I... am looking at that beauty, again and again,
with passion to embrace me with her perfume and
some fear, not to hurt her.

Ernesto Kahan © 7/1/2017

*翻譯成西班牙語詩

Mingli,

Eres mi representación de sana juventud,

La sonrisa que atrapa al día para no soltarlo,

Manos pintando la vida imaginada,

Una boca pronunciando las mágicas palabras

Para la bella y amada poesía humana.

Flor en la hierba que amanece después de la lluvia

Y que yo miro, una y otra vez, con temor a lastimarla

Y con pasión para abrazarme a su perfume

Ernesto Kahan © 7/1/2017

2.以色列著名醫師詩人 Prof.Ernesto Kahan 翻譯林明理詩作（海影）成西班牙語（Israel poet Prof.Ernesto Kahan translating Lin Mingli poems （OCEAN REFLECTION) into Spanish）

Re: Reflejo del océano por Lin Mingli Traducido del inglés por Ernesto Kahan

Prof.Ernesto Kahan 於2016.2.4MAIL 1:46 PM 翻譯了林明理的詩作（海影）成西班牙語

2. 海影

*林明理

第一次被你感動
我很難說清
在你燦爛的光痕
我以為世上並無如此美好的真情
是風的呼喚
讓我們因緣際會
想讓你認出了我

就忘了國與國的距離
有什麼差別

當我喜愛這一切——
棕櫚樹和沙灘、詩集
音樂
啊，島嶼一望無際
如何能留住你的身影
月亮啊，請不要再多說
我只信眼前所聞
一次相遇肯定不夠
在灰藍、灰藍的星群上
明天，請為我們打開希望之門

　註：作者於二〇一三年十月下旬參訪馬來西亞第三十三屆
世詩會，看到各國國旗並列於海面上，蘇丹王子及州長、市長、
諾貝爾獎得主 Dr.kahan 等名人前來祝辭，有感而文。
　－刊臺灣（人間福報）副刊，2013.11.18.

海影

文／林明理

第一次被你感動
我很難說清
在你燦爛的光暈
我以為世上並無如此美好的真情
是風的呼喚
讓我們因緣際會
想讓你認出了我
就忘了國與國的距離
有什麼差別

當我喜愛這一切——
棕櫚樹和沙灘、詩集
音樂

阿，島嶼一望無際
如何能留住你的身影
月亮阿，請不要再多說
我只信眼前所聞
一次相遇肯定不夠
在灰藍、友藍的星群上
明天，請為我們打開希望之門

註：作者於二○一三年十月下旬參訪馬來西亞第三十三屆世詩會，看到各國國旗並列於海面上，蘇丹王子及州長、市長、諾貝爾獎得主Dr.kihan等名人前來祝辭，有感而文。

奇觀。看完沉船，我們便駛往花瓶島看花瓶岩，一部分遊客登島參觀，我們只有行程而未登島，從船上開心欣賞島上的天然美景之餘，沒忘了在靠近花瓶岩時全

詩賞注「諦聽」這旦岩是白灰灰兩塊岩，美感比不上台灣野柳附

小石片的地點，尋尋覓覓地不可得，好一陣唏然若失之感。但硬幣之石仍象難以抹滅。要說那是古文明遺物嗎？或許更正確的說法是老天爺的口袋破了個小洞，無意間散落下來的一天幣」吧。

可以把那些瓶瓶罐罐一拿下來，像欣賞化妝品似地嗅聞、閱讀它們的用途、產地。

中國式香料，最常用在滷味角、陳皮、花椒與糖、醬油、酒水調配，做留學生時，沒事滷一大鍋分好幾餐吃，人人都拿手。還有茶葉蛋，我自己愛慣不用市面上的茶葉蛋滷包，怕味道太重，喧賓

2.Reflejo del océano por Lin Mingli

La primera vez que me conmoví por ti
no fui capaz de responder con claridad.
Eras luz, magnífica;
la cosa más bella en el mundo,
el llamado del viento
para reconocerte en su oportunidad
y olvidar las diferencias
entre naciones

Amo a todos esos —
las palmeras y la playa
libros de poesía y música
Oh, ¿cómo puede la gran isla
mantener su figura?
Oh luna, no digas más
Confío en lo que veo
y un sólo encuentro no es bastante.
Por encima de las estrellas de azul-gris,
ábrenos mañana la puerta de la esperanza

Traducido del inglés por Ernesto Kahan / 西班牙語

2. OCEAN REFLECTION

by Lin Mingli

The first time I was moved by you
I was not able to say it clearly
In your magnificent light
I thought there was no such beautiful thing in the world
It was the calling of the wind
that led me to recognize you at the opportune moment
and to forget the differences
between nations

And I love all of these--
the palm trees and the beach
books of poetry and music
O, how can the vast island
hold your figure
O moon, please say no more
I only trust what I see
One encounter is evidently not enough
Above the blue-gray stars
tomorrow, please open for us the door of hope

(Translated by William. Marr　美國名詩人非馬 英譯)

六、附錄 appendix

1. 散文兩篇 Two essays

(1) 母子情　＊林明理

　　阿桃的孩子出生時，因腦缺氧太久，成了智障兒，眼力也有些受損。知道事實後，原本貧困的她，連悲哀的時間都沒有了，只能更賣命地做活，含辛茹苦地把小孩拉把長大，這是她唯一能為他做的一件事。不過，這孩子很孝順，儘管在求學過程中困難重重，但從不氣餒，反而常常安慰為他日夜擔憂的母親。

　　阿桃對孩子的期待不多，最大的希望是要他平安健康、順利地學得一技之長，可以用自己的力量活下去。難得的是，這小孩從小就會把家裡打掃得乾淨，也對別人很有禮貌。多年後，當他從私立高工建教班畢業前的一個早上，興奮地從學校撥了電話回家：「媽媽，我得到市長獎，也通過證照考試啦！」阿桃掛上電話的那一剎那，頻頻拭淚，讓歡喜的淚水滴在她粗糙的手背上。當她告訴我時，聲音充滿了笑意，她那多皺紋的面孔一下子變得那麼舒展了。但不知為什麼，我有著欲淚的激動。

是呀，親情間最容易忽略的「愛」，在這對母子身上卻很容易地表達出來。她對孩子從不放棄希望，而她的小孩也終能克服障礙，努力學得專長，活出快樂的自己。

－2017.9.6 作

－刊美國〈亞特蘭大新聞〉，亞城園地版， 2017.10.6.

（2）物理界怪傑－周建和教授　　*林明理

十年前，我毅然辭去大學教職，重拾文筆不久，身體條件很差，所以就常到鄰近的公園運動。當時，周建和教授是我同道拳友。一晃眼，已過許多年了。日前，我在歸途的火車上一眼看到他，就熱絡地打招呼，坐在一起開始聊天了起來。

印象中，建和兄喜歡理個大平頭、悠閒地騎著鐵馬，晃到公園來習拳。第一次看到他與周建新教授在樹蔭下聊天時，我對他的目光如炬、一臉聰明相又有本土音的這位高師大教授特別地感到好奇。

那年，過年期間，他很熱心地開車，邀請拳友們一起到他的學校附近的泥火山遊玩；還當場教大家動手作紙片螺旋槳實驗，很有趣。後來，我們也與拳友們登山踏青，他喜歡穿著短褲、長襪、登山帽、鞋，再背上大背包，十足像個前往尋寶的考古學家。誰知道這號人物，竟是個物理學術界的怪傑！

記得有一天清晨，他手裡握著一張「人間福報」，低聲地告訴我：「明理，妳的文章刊出來啦！」我一臉興奮地謝謝他，教練也趕緊把這張報紙張貼在公佈欄白板上，以示鼓勵。自此，我便開展我的文學寫作之旅。

當我在網路搜尋到建和兄的簡介，才知道在浩瀚的宇宙深處，年過半白的他，畢生都在推行及演講物理生活化的運動。

他擅長利用科學魔術或神奇實驗，以遊戲和競賽的活潑教學，讓學習物理變得簡單又有實用性。我發現，在視覺的實驗過程中，他已把物理觀念悄悄滲入物象，完成了許多難以理解的原理。

我覺得，一個真正悟解宇宙奧祕的科學家或學者，放眼自然，所做的事應當皆是有深慧的哲理。如果你跟他結緣，親眼目睹他在教人動手做做看時的認真態度及幽默的表情，你就可以體會其中的樂趣。除了教學外，建和兄也與求學時期的好友與同好，共同催生了「街頭物理」的計畫。不論是公園的大樹下、或文化中心前廣場、愛河畔或中小學等地，都是他們的推廣據點。在推動街頭物理十餘年後，他有感於偏鄉地區在科普教育的學習資源上較為缺乏，遂而將街頭物理的觸角延伸至偏鄉學校。所以，他也是「山區特色科普教材之開發設計」計畫主持人。最近幾年來，都與其它教師默默地付出他們的心血，讓指導的學生們明白教育的責任及勇於付出的喜悅。

臨別前，我悄悄地問建和兄，有那個國小在教學時，是印象最深刻的？他不加思索地告訴我，是大鞍國小！那是一所位於南投竹山鎮山區的迷你小學，創校卻已超過一甲子。校區擁有孟宗林、櫻花、肖楠、紅檜等珍貴資產，所以又有「被遺忘的綠色珍珠」之美譽。建和兄津津樂道地說，由於山區的冬筍筍價是其他季節的十倍，是當地重要的經濟作物。他的團對經由科學探究，讓學童瞭解竹子生態特性，並應用物理與生物知識，發展出高效率挖冬筍科學方法，也教會了學童防災知識的建立與科學能力的培養。

此外，建和兄還邀集了具有動手做科普經驗的學者與老師、和山區國小教師組成團隊，以山區自然環境、特色產業、生活為題材與資源，開發具有特色的科普教材，例如「大鞍國小太陽能行動」、「大鞍山區的礦物世界」、以及「雲霧的觀察與產生」等等，並安排小小解說員到其它國小進行科普活動的交流。據説，這項科普教育活動，讓大鞍國小全校學生從數年前的九人增加到將近四十人。

　　此刻，想起建和兄説的每一細節，每一個與學童的教學畫面……我看到了一群志同道合的科學人的勇氣與堅持。因為他們有了對教育偏遠學童更需要付出的執著，才有了這樣的勇氣。一次萍聚，雖然只有匆匆的兩個多小時，但這次的偶遇便在時光的脈絡裡多留下一份感動。我深信他們的努力終會使生命變得更曠達、更豐盈！

--2017.4.27

林明理 / 畫作　Dr.Lin
Mingli paint work

刊臺灣（台灣時報），台灣文學版，2017.5.3，圖文。

頒獎狀於 2017 年 4 月 21 日。Lin Ming-Li won the Italian (International Reading Committee) award on April 21, 2017.

義大利詩人出版家 Giovanni Campisi 於 2017/6/15 (週四) 5:00 PM MAIL MINGLI：

Hereby the IPN with the list of Nobel Prize candidates-Let me know what you think about it (2)

－刊登於 2017.6.12 義大利 出版的《國際詩新聞》。

　　*義大利的（國際閱讀委員會），特聘 EDIZIONI Universum
選擇來自歐洲和歐洲以外的發表作品提交入圍 2018 年諾貝爾
文學獎候選人名單的一個參考選擇。其中包括林明理 2017 年
在台北市出版的文學專著《我的歌》。

　　* Italian (International Reading Committee), Distinguished
EDIZIONI Universum selected works from outside Europe and
Europe to submit a list of nominations for the 2018 Nobel Prize
for Literature. Including Lin Mingli published in Taipei City in
2017 literary monograph [my song].

1. Ming-Li Lin con il libro di
poesie in cinese, inglese, francese
e spagnolo
MY SONG

SPRING
非歐洲 POETS
1.林明理的書
詩歌，英語，法語
和西班牙語
我的歌

　　2017年義大利出版的女詩人 SARA CIAMPI 詩集的封面採用林明理此畫作。義大利 Giovanni 出版，2017.04 義大利女詩人 Sara Ciampi 譯詩集《時代的片斷》《FRAGMENTS OF TIME》書封面採用林明理的水彩畫作〈臺灣日出〉.

　　2017 Italian published poet SARA CIAMPI poetry cover, the use of Lin Ming Li this painting.

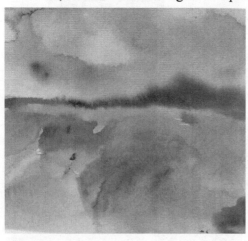

林明理　畫/ Lin Ming-Li Paint

2. 林明理的中、英、法文簡介及專著
Dr. Lin Mingli's Chinese, English and French profiles and monographs

林明理 Dr.Lin Ming-Li 簡介

　　林明理，1961 年生，臺灣雲林縣人，中國文化大學大陸問題研究所法學碩士，美國世界文化藝術學院榮譽文學博士（2013.10.21 頒授）。曾任屏東師範學院講師，現任中國文藝協會理事、中華民國新詩學會理事，北京「國際漢語詩歌協會」理事，詩人評論家。2013.5.4獲第 54 屆「中國文藝獎章」文學類「詩歌創作獎」。2012. 9.9.人間衛視『知道』節目專訪林明理 1 小時，播出於第 110 集「以詩與畫追夢的心─林明理」。台灣「文化部」贊助，民視『飛越文學地景』拍攝林明理三首詩作錄影（白冷圳之戀）（2017.7.15 民視新聞首播）、〈歌飛阿里山森林〉（2016.12.24 民視新聞首播）、〈寫給蘭嶼之歌〉

（2016.11.19 民視新聞首播）。著有《秋收的黃昏》、《夜櫻--詩畫集》、《新詩的意象與內涵--當代詩家作品賞析》、《藝術與自然的融合--當代詩文評論集》、《湧動著一泓清泉─現代詩文評論》、《用詩藝開拓美─林明理談詩》、《林明理報刊評論》、《行走中的歌者─林明理談詩》、《海頌─林明理詩文集》、《林明理散文集》、《名家現代詩賞析》。以及詩集《山楂樹》、《回憶的沙漏》（中英對照）、《清雨塘》（中英對照）、《山居歲月》（中英對照）、《夏之吟》（中英法對照）、《默喚》（中英法對照）、《我的歌》（中法對照）。她的詩畫被收錄編於山西大學新詩研究所 2015 年編著《當代著名漢語詩人詩書畫檔案》、詩作六首被收錄於《雲林縣青少年臺灣文學讀本》，評論作品被碩士生研究引用數十篇論文，作品包括詩畫、散文與評論散見於海內外學刊及詩刊、報紙等。中國學報刊物包括有《南京師範大學文學院學報》、《青島師範學院學報》、《鹽城師範學報》等二十多篇，臺灣的國圖刊物《全國新書資訊月刊》二十六篇，還有在中國大陸的詩刊報紙多達五十種刊物發表，如《天津文學》、《安徽文學》、《香港文學》等。在臺灣《人間福報》已發表上百篇作品，在《臺灣時報》、《笠詩刊》與《秋水詩刊》等刊物也常發表作品，另外，在美國的刊物《世界的詩》或報紙《亞特蘭大新聞》等也有發表作品。總計發表的創作與評論作品已達千篇以上。

　　Dr. Lin Ming-Li was born in 1961 in Yunlin, Taiwan. She holds a Master's Degree in Law and lectured at Pingtung Normal College. A poetry critic, she is currently serving as a director of the Chinese Literature and Art Association, the Chinese New Poetry Society, and Beijing's International Association of Chinese Poetry. On the 4th of May, 2013, she won the Creative Poetry Prize in the 54th Chinese Literature and Arts Awards. On the 21st of October 2013, she received a Doctor of Literature degree from America's World Culture and Art Institute. On the 9th of September 2012, the World Satellite TV Station in Taiwan broadcast her interview, "Lin Ming-Li: The Heart that Pursues a Dream with Poetry and Painting". FTV (FORMOSA TELEVISION) videoed three poems by her, namely, "Love of the Bethlehem Ditch" (2017.07.15 premiere)."Songs Fill the Forest of Mt. Ali " (2016.12.24 premiere) and "Ode to the Orchid Island" (2016.11.19 premiere).

　　Her publications include *An Autumn Harvest Evening, Night Sakura: Collection of Poems and Paintings, Images and Connotations of New Poetry :*

Reading and Analysis of the Works of Contemporary Poets, The Fusing of Art and Nature: Criticism of Contemporary Poetry and Literature, The Gushing of a Pure Spring: Modern Poetry Criticism, Developing Beauty with Poetic Art: Lin Ming-Li On Poetry, A Collection of Criticism from Newspapers and Magazines, The Walking Singer: Lin Ming-Li On Poetry, Ode to the Sea: A Collection of Poems and Essays of Lin Ming-Li, Appreciation of the Work of Famous Modern Poets, and *Lin Ming-Li's Collected Essays.*

Her poems were anthologized in *Hawthorn Tree, Memory's Hourglass,* (Chinese/English), *Clear Rain Pond* (Chinese/English), *Days in the Mountains* (Chinese/English), *Summer Songs* (Chinese/English/French) , *Silent Call* (Chinese/English/French) and *My song* (Chinese/French).

Many of her poems and paintings are collected in *A Collection of Poetry, Calligraphy and Painting by Contemporary Famous Chinese Poets,* compiled in 2015 by New Poetry Research Institute of Shanxi University. Six of her poems are included in *Taiwanese Literary Textbook for the Youth of Yunlin County.* Her review articles have been quoted in theses by many graduate students. Over a thousand of her works, including poems, paintings, essays, and criticisms have appeared in many newspapers and academic journals at home and abroad.

Le Docteur Lin Ming-Li est née en 1961 à Yunlin, Taïwan. Titulaire d'une maîtrise en droit, elle a été maître de conférences à l'École Normale de Pingtung. Critique de poésie, elle occupe actuellement le poste d'administrateur de l'Association Art et Littérature chinois, de l'Association Nouvelle Poésie chinoise et de l'Association internationale de poésie chinoise de Pékin. Le 4 mai 2013, elle a obtenu le Prix de Poésie créative lors du 54e palmarès de littérature et d'art chinois. Le 21 octobre 2013, l'Institut de la Culture et des Arts du Monde d'Amérique lui a attribué le titre de Docteur. Le 9 septembre 2012, la Station Mondiale de télévision par satellite de Taiwan a diffusé une interview d'elle intitulée « Lin Ming-Li, le cœur qui poursuit ses rêves par la Poésie et la Peinture ». «Célèbre poésie moderne Appréciation». " Lin Ming-Li Collected Essays ".FTV (FORMOSA TELEVISION) vidéo LIN MING-LI deux poèmes"Love of the Bethlehem Ditch" (2017.07.15 première). (chansons volent Alishan

Forest) (2016.12.24 première) et (Orchid a écrit la chanson) (Première 2016.11.19).

Ses publications comprennent les titres suivants : « Soir de moisson d'automne », « Nuit des Cerisiers -   recueil de poèmes et de peintures »,   « Images et connotations de la Nouvelle Poésie - lecture et analyse des œuvres de poètes contemporains », « Fusion de l'Art et de la Nature - critique sur la Poésie et la Littérature contemporaines »,   « Le Jaillissement d'une source pure – étude sur la poésie moderne », « Rehaussement de la Beauté grâce à l'Art poétique - Lin Ming-Li au sujet de la poésie », « Recueil de critiques tirées de journaux et de revues », « Les Chanteurs errants - Lin Ming-Li au sujet de la poésie » et « Ode à la mer – recueil de poèmes et d'essais de Lin Ming-Li ». Ses autres livres de poésie sont : « L'Aubépine », « La clepsydre de la mémoire » (bilingue : chinois – anglais), « L'Étang de pluie claire » (bilingue : chinois – anglais), « Jours passés dans les montagnes » (bilingue : chinois – anglais), « Chants d'été » (trilingue : chinois – anglais – français) et « L'appel silencieux » (trilingue : chinois – anglais – français) , «Ma poésie» (trilingue : chinois – français) .

.

Certains de ses poèmes et peintures figurent dans le « *Recueil de poésies, calligraphies et peintures des plus notables poètes chinois contemporains* » publié en 2015 par l'Institut de Recherches sur la nouvelle poésie de l'Université de Shanxi.

Six de ses poésies figurent dans le « *Manuel de littérature taïwanaise pour la jeunesse du comté de Yunlin* ». Ses articles publiés dans différents magazines ont été cités dans les thèses de nombreux diplômés. Des milliers de ses œuvres de poésie, de peinture, d'essai et de critique ont eu l'honneur des colonnes de revues et journaux du monde entier.

林明理博士得獎等事項記錄：

1.2011 年臺灣「國立高雄應用科技大學 詩歌類評審」校長聘書。

2.詩畫作品獲收入中國文聯 2015.01 出版「當代著名漢語詩人詩書畫檔案」一書，山西當代中國新詩研究所主編。

3.2015.1.2 受邀重慶市研究生科研創新專案重點項目「中國臺灣新詩生態調查及文體研究」，訪談內文刊於湖南文聯《創作與評論》2015.02。

4.《中國今世詩歌導讀》編委會、國際詩歌翻譯研討中心等主辦，獲《中國今世詩歌獎（2011-2012）指摘獎》第 7 名。

5.獲 2013 年中國文藝協會與安徽省淮安市淮陰區人民政府主辦，"漂母杯"兩岸「母愛主題」散文大賽第三等獎。2014"漂母杯"兩岸「母愛主題」散文大賽第三等獎、詩歌第二等獎。2015"漂母杯"兩岸「母愛主題」詩歌第二等獎。

6.新詩〈歌飛霍山茶鄉〉獲得安徽省「霍山黃茶」杯全國原創詩歌大賽組委會「榮譽獎」榮譽證書。

7.參加中國河南省開封市文學藝術聯合會「全國詠菊詩歌創作大賽」，榮獲銀獎證書〈2012.12.18 公告〉，詩作〈詠菊之鄉─開封〉。

8."湘家蕩之戀"國際散文詩徵文獲榮譽獎，散文詩作品：〈寫給相湖的歌〉，嘉興市湘家蕩區域開發建設管理委員會、中外散文詩學會舉辦，2014.9.28 頒獎於湘家蕩。

9.獲當選中國北京「國際漢語詩歌協會」理事〈2013-2016〉。

10.獲當選中國第 15 屆「全國散文詩筆會」臺灣代表，甘肅舉辦「吉祥甘南」全國散文詩大賽，獲「提名獎」，2015.7.26 頒獎於甘南，詩作〈甘南，深情地呼喚我〉，詩作刊於**《散文詩·校園文學》甘南采風專號 2015.12（總第 422 期）**及《格桑花》2015"吉祥甘南"全國散文詩筆會專號。

11.2015.08 中國·星星「月河月老」杯（兩岸三地）愛情散文詩大賽獲「優秀獎」，詩作〈月河行〉。

12.北京新視野杯"我與自然"全國散文詩歌大賽獲獎於 2015.10
獲散文〈布農布落遊蹤〉及詩歌〈葛根塔拉草原之戀〉均「二等獎」。

13.河南省2015年8月首屆"中國詩河 鶴壁"全國詩歌大賽,獲「提
名獎」,詩作〈寫給鶴壁的歌〉。

14.2015.9 中央廣播電臺、河南省中共鄭州市委宣傳部主辦"待月
嵩山 2015 中秋詩會詩歌大賽"獲三等獎,新詩作品〈嵩山之夢〉,
獲人民幣 1 千元獎金及獎狀。

15.2012 年 9 月 9 日人間衛視『知道』節目專訪林明理 1 小時,
播 出 於 第 110 集 「 以 詩 與 畫 追 夢 的 心 — 林 明 理 」 。
http://www.bltv.tv/program/?f=content&sid=170&cid=6750

16. 雲林縣政府編印,主持人成功大學陳益源教授,《雲林縣青
少年臺灣文學讀本》新詩卷,2016.04 出版,收錄林明理新詩六首,
(九份黃昏)(行經木棧道)(淡水紅毛城)(雨,落在愛河的冬
夜)(生命的樹葉)(越過這個秋季)於頁 215-225。

17.北京,2015 年全國詩書畫家創作年會,林明理新詩(夢見中
國)獲「二等獎」,頒獎典禮在 2015.12.26 人民大會堂賓館舉行。

18.福建省邵武市,2015.12.15 公告,文體廣電新聞出版局主辦,
邵武"張三豐杯海內外詩歌大賽",林明理新詩〈邵武戀歌〉獲「優秀
獎」。

19.安徽詩歌學會主辦,肥東縣文聯承辦,第二屆"曹植詩歌獎"
華語詩歌大賽,林明理獲二等獎,獎狀及獎金人民幣兩千,2016.3.28
中 國 煤 炭 新 聞 網 公 告 。
http://www.cwestc.com/newshtml/2016-4-2/406808.shtml

http://www.myyoco.com/folder2288/folder2290/folder2292/2016/0
4/2016-04-22706368.html 來源:肥東縣人民政府網站 發佈時間:
2016-04-22。詩作(〈寫給曹植之歌〉外一首)刊於中共肥東縣委宣
傳網 http://www.fdxcb.gov.cn/display.asp?id=37800

20.北京市寫作學會等主辦,2016 年"東方美"全國詩聯書畫大
賽,新詩(頌長城),榮獲「金獎」。

21. 2016"源泉之歌"全國詩歌大賽,林明理新詩(寫給成都之歌)
獲 優 秀 獎 , 中 國 (華 西 都 市 報) 2016.6.16 公 告 於
http://www.kaixian.tv/gd/2016/0616/568532.html

22.2016.11.19 民視新聞（FORMOSA TELEVISION）下午三點五十七分首播（飛閱文學地景）節目林明理吟誦（寫給蘭嶼之歌）。
https://www.youtube.com/watch?v=F95ruijjXfE
　　https://v.qq.com/x/page/e0350zb01ay.html 騰訊視頻
　　http://www.atlantachinesenews.com/ 2016.12.2 美國（亞特蘭大新聞）刊
　　民視【飛閱文學地景】林明理吟詩（寫給蘭嶼之歌）於首頁網，可點播
　　http://videolike.org/video/%E9%A3%9B%E9%96%B1%E6%96%87%E5%AD%B8%E5%9C%B0%E6%99%AF 【飛閱文學地景】video
　　https://www.facebook.com/WenHuaBu/posts/1174239905989277
台灣的「文化部」臉書
23.2016.12.24 民視新聞晚上六點首播（飛閱文學地景）節目林明理吟誦（歌飛阿里山森林）。
　　https://www.youtube.com/watch?v=3KAq4xKxEZM
　　http://www.woplay.net/watch?v=3KAq4xKxEZM
24.詩作（夏之吟），2015.1.2 應邀於《海星詩刊》舉辦【翰墨詩香】活動於台北市長官邸藝文中心聯展。
　　詩作（那年冬夜），2017.2.4 應邀於《海星詩刊》舉辦【詩的影像】活動於台北市長官邸藝文中心聯展。
　　http://cloud.culture.tw/frontsite/inquiry/eventInquiryAction.do?method=showEventDetail&uid=586f3b1acc46d8fa6452ca16 文化部網
25.義大利（國際閱讀委員會）（international Reading Committee）頒獎狀給林明理於 2017.04.21.
26.2017.7.15 民視新聞 FTV（Taiwan Formosa live news HD）晚上六點首播（飛閱文學地景）節目林明理吟誦（白冷圳之戀）。
　　https://www.youtube.com/watch?v=6b17mmHQG3Q
　　http://videolike.org/view/yt=f2pgDDqzScz
27. 林明理散文作品（寫給包公故里－肥東），獲 2017 年第三屆中國包公散文獎徵文比賽 B 組散文詩三等獎，收編入中共安徽省肥東縣宣傳部，肥東縣文聯舉辦，第三屆"中國•包公散文獎"獲獎作品集，【中國散文之鄉】。

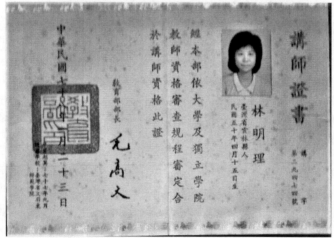

林 明 理 專 書
Dr.Lin Mingli'smonograph

1.《秋收的黃昏》The evening of autumn。高雄市：春暉出版社，2008。

2.《夜櫻-林明理詩畫集》Cherry Blossoms at Night。高雄市：春暉出版社，2009。

3.《新詩的意象與內涵-當代詩家作品賞析》The Imagery and Connetation of New Poetry-A Collection of Critical Poetry Analysis。臺北市：文津出版社，2010。

4.《藝術與自然的融合-當代詩文評論集》The Fusion Of Art and Nature。臺北市：文史哲出版社，2011。

5.《山楂樹》HAWTHORN Poems by Lin Mingli（林明理詩集）。臺北市：文史哲出版社，2011。

6.《回憶的沙漏》（中英對照譯詩集）Sandglass Of Memory。臺北市：秀威出版社，2012。

7.《湧動著一泓清泉一現代詩文評論》A GUSHING SPRING-A COLLECTION OF C O M M E N T S O N MODERN LITERARY WORKS。臺北市：文史哲出版社，2012。

8.《清雨塘》Clear Rain Pond（中英對照譯詩集）。臺北市：文史哲出版社，2012。

9.《用詩藝開拓美—林明理讀詩》DEVELOPING BEAUTY THOUGH THE ART OF POETRY – Lin Mingli On Poetry。臺北市：秀威出版社，2013。

10.《海頌—林明理詩文集》Hymn To the Ocean（poems and Essays）。臺北市：文史哲出版社，2013。

11.《林明理報刊評論 1990-2000》Published Commentaries1990-2000。臺北市：文史哲出版社，2013。

12.《行走中的歌者—林明理談詩》The Walking singer-Ming-Li Lin On Poetry。臺北市：文史哲出版社，2013。

13.《山居歲月》Days in the Mountains（中英對照譯詩集）。臺北市：文史哲出版社，2015。

14.《夏之吟》Summer Songs（中英法譯詩集）。英譯：馬為義（筆名：非馬）（William Marr）。法譯：阿薩納斯 · 薩拉西（Athanase Vantchev de Thracy）。法國巴黎：索倫紮拉文化學院（The Cultural Institute of Solenzara），2015。

15.《默喚》Silent Call(中英法譯詩集)。英譯：諾頓 · 霍奇斯（Norton Hodges）。法譯：阿薩納斯 · 薩拉西（Athanase Vantchev de Thracy）。法國巴黎：索倫紮拉文化學院（The Cultural Institute of Solenzara），2016。

16.《林明理散文集》Lin Ming Li´s Collected essays。臺北市：文史哲出版社，2016。

17.《名家現代詩賞析》Appreciation of the work of Famous Modern Poets。臺北市：文史哲出版社，2016。

18.《我的歌　MY SONG》，Athanase Vantchev de Thracy 中法譯詩集。臺北市：文史哲出版 社，2017。

19.《諦聽 Listen》，（中英對照譯詩集）。英譯：馬為義（筆名：非馬）（William Marr）。臺北市：文史哲出版社，2018。

Dr. Lin Ming-Li
默　喚
Silent Call - L'appel silencieux

◎林明理 著　◎法譯 - Athanase Vantchev
de Thracy – français
◎英譯 Norton Hodges – English

Éditions Institut Culturel de Solenzara

林明理散文集
LIN MING-LI'S COLLECTED ESSAYS

林明理 著　author：Dr.Lin Ming-Li

文 學 叢 刊
文史哲出版社印行

名家現代詩賞析
Appreciation of the work of Famous Modern Poets

林明理 著　author：Dr.Lin Ming-Li

現代文學研究叢刊
文史哲出版社印行

我 的 歌
My Song

林明理 著　Dr. AthanaseVantchev
Dr. Lin Mingli author　de Thracy-français 法譯

文 學 叢 刊
文史哲出版社印行

文史哲中英對照叢刊

諦 聽
中英對照詩集
Listen
Poetry Collection (Chinese & English)

林明理 著　非馬（馬為義）譯
Author: Dr. Lin Mingli　Translator: Dr. William Marr

諦聽

林明理 著

非馬（馬為義）譯

文史哲英漢叢刊
The Liberal Arts Press

文史哲出版社印行

Lin Ming-Li, short CV

Dr. Lin Ming-Li was born in
1961 in Yunlin, Taiwan. She
holds a Master's Degree in Law
and tutored at Pingtung Normal
College. A poetry critic, she is
currently serving as a director of
the Chinese Literature and Art
Association, the Chinese New
Poetry Society, and Beijing's
International Association of
Chinese Poetry. On the 14th of
May, 2013, she won the Creative Poetry Prize in the 55th
Chinese Literature and Arts Awards. On the 21st of
October 2013, she received a Doctor of Literature degree
from America's World Culture and Art Institute. On the
9th of September 2015, the World Satellite TV Station in
Taiwan broadcast her interview, "Lin Ming-Li: The Heart
that Pursues Dreams with Poem and Painting". On the
22nd of August, 2104, FTV (FORMOSA TELEVISION)
videoed her poems by her, namely, "Songs Fill the Forest
of Mt. Ali "(2016.12.24 poems) and "Ode to the Orchid
Island" (2016.12.39 poems) - "Love of the Bethlehem
Ditch" (2017.07.15 poems).

She has a total of 18 books on literature and poetry. Is
currently a poet, a poet critic, good at painting. Commen-
tary works are cited by dozens of papers by graduate
students.

林明理，一九六一年生於台灣雲林縣。
法學碩士，曾任屏東師範學院講師。
現任中國文藝協會理事、中國詩歌藝術
學會理事、北京「國際漢語詩歌協會」
理事等職。二○一三年五月十四日獲第
五十五屆中國文藝獎章文學創作獎詩
歌獎。二○一三年十月二十一日獲美國
世界文化藝術學院榮譽文學博士。二○
一五年九月九日台灣「國家網路電視」
錄影林明理訪談節目「以詩與畫追夢
的心——林明理」。二○一四年八月二
十二日台灣「民視」錄影林明理的詩作
——「阿里山森林之歌」（2016.12.24詩
作）、「蘭嶼頌」（2016.12.39詩作）——
「愛是伯利恆之溝」（2017.07.15詩作）。

林明理著有文學及詩集共十八冊。現為
詩人、詩評家、善繪畫。評論作品被數
十位研究生的論文所引用。

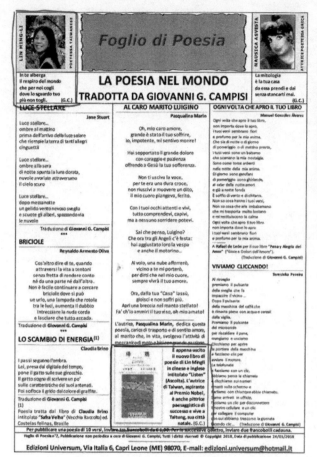

林明理 LIN MINGLI 台灣女人 POETESSA TAIWANESE

In te alberga
il respiro del mondo
che per noi cogli
dove lo sguardo tuo
più non togli. (G.C.)

È appena uscito il nuovo libro di poesie di Lin Mingli in cinese e inglese intitolato "Listen" (Ascolta). L'autrice di Taiwan, aspirante al Premio Nobel, è anche pittrice paesaggistica di successo e vive a Taitung, sua città natale. (G.C.)

她剛出版
新書
Lin Mingli 的詩
用中文和英文
題為"諦聽"LISTEN。
作者住台灣,有被提名
名單到諾貝爾獎,
她也是一個畫家,
成功地美化生活於
台東－她住的城市,
是在地人。

. . . .

義大利【國際詩新聞】2018.1.24 報導
於名詩人 Giovanni Campisi───→

有您眞好
——給彭正雄大哥

所有我的大部份作品和
　那些詩畫
都在您的巧手製作下
編輯成美麗的書
興奮的我像頑皮的孩子
　將把它們緊抱在我的胸膛

——2018.1.25感謝文史哲出版家彭正雄
先生為我製作此書，明理合十。

Nice to have you
— Peng Zhengxiong brother
*Dr.Lin Mingli

Most of my works and
　Those poetry and painting
Under your skilled production
Edited into a beautiful book
I am excited like a naughty child
　Will hold them tight in my chest

——2018.1.25 Thank you Mr. Wenzheng Peng
publisher for making this book for me.

七、後 記

感謝美國詩人非馬（馬為義博士 Dr.William Marr）在 2017 年為我翻譯英詩及鼓勵，也感謝天津師範大學外國語文系張智中教授、以色列醫師詩人 prof.Ernesto Kahan、法國詩人 Athanase Vantchev de Thracy、義大利詩人 Giovanni Campisi 的翻譯。最後再次向文史哲出版家彭正雄先生、及彭雅雲女士為本書所付出的辛勞致意。

Postscript

Thanked the American poet for Dr. William Marr in 2017 for my translation of English poetry and encouragement, also thanks to Tianjin Normal University Department of Foreign Languages Professor Zhang Zhizhong, Israel physician poet prof.Ernesto Kahan, French poet Athanase Vantchev de Thracy, Italian poet Giovanni Campisi translation. Finally, once again to Xiuwei information issuer Mr. Song Zhengkun, deputy editor Cai Dengshan and responsible editor of a gentleman, graphic layout of a lady, the cover design of a lady for the book to pay the hard work to pay tribute. And finally to the literary history of the publisher Mr. Peng Cheng-hisung, and Ms. Peng Yayun for the book to pay the hard work to pay tribute.

林明理　Dr.Lin　Mingli　in
Taiwan　Taitung　2018.01.01.